"I have endeavored to create...a knitting book which is like no other; one which is at once practical, unique, of interest to both beginning and advanced knitters—and most of all, easy."*

To test her theories of teaching knitting the simple way, needlework expert, Barbara Aytes, enlisted the aid of two friends—one a slightly experienced knitter, the other a total stranger to the art. It is their tasteful, attractive creations that are shown in the book's 122 photographs. Working only from the directions in this book, they became expert knitters without asking a single question or dropping a single stitch!

*From the Preface

D0034437

KNITTING MADE EASY
was originally published by
Doubleday & Company, Inc.

Also by Barbara Aytes

Adventures in Knitting

 *Are there paperbound books you want
but cannot find in your retail stores?*

KNITTING
Made Easy

Barbara Aytes

PUBLISHED BY POCKET BOOKS NEW YORK

Photography by Jerome Shapiro

Fashion Model: Dede Boggs

Floral Motif and Alternate Floral Motif in Chapter 6 and Diamond
Weave Pattern in Chapter 7 were originally designed by the author
for use in fashion items for Spinnerin Yarn Company, Inc., and it is
with their permission that these patterns are used herein.

KNITTING MADE EASY

Doubleday edition published March, 1970
Pocket Book edition published April, 1971

This *Pocket Book* edition includes every word
contained in the original, higher-priced edition. It is printed
from brand-new plates made from completely reset, clear, easy-to-read
type. *Pocket Book* editions are published by Pocket Books, a division
of Simon & Schuster, Inc., 630 Fifth Avenue, New York, N.Y. 10020.
Trademarks registered in the United States and other countries.

1 2 3 4 5 2 1 0

Contents

Part Two:

DECORATIVE MOTIFS

Part Three:

LACY AND ELEGANT PATTERNS

Part Four:

FLOWER CARD DIAGRAMS

CHAPTER 10

Preface

A knitted item requiring very little or no shaping and made in only two or three pieces often contains all the elements of good taste which all knitters wish to achieve, but which many believe come from complicated shaping, many parts, and constant referral to long and intricate directions. Nothing could be further from the truth.

As a general rule, the finished item appears non-professional and inelegant the more complicated the style and the more pieces comprising it. Occasionally, it creates an overall illusion of poor taste and careless planning, when in fact the item in question may have been carefully planned, laboriously shaped, and lovingly put together.

Both beginning knitters and more advanced knitters who refuse to waste their time on much-too-complicated directions have the ability to create beautiful hand-knitted items that are simple and elegant. It is for these kindred souls that this book was written. A simple knitted square or rectangle of fabric, with little or no shaping, can be used in a myriad of ways, in exactly the same manner as the well-known "basic black" dress can be varied or embellished ad infinitum, so that it appears to be many fashions. For example, the simplest garment I have ever designed, a cap-sleeve blouse, has also proved to be the most popular. It can be knitted in endless variations and is casual and elegant in a way that is difficult to duplicate by more complicated techniques. It consists simply of two knitted rectangles with no shaping whatsoever. Once started, it requires no further reference to directions until the upper edge is bound off. When made with a medium-weight yarn, the time it takes to complete is amazingly short.

In the first five chapters I have given all the basics, with step-by-step instructions, which the beginner, with a little practice, should have no trouble in executing. Each group of basic stitches and techniques in each chapter is followed by directions for simple items which the beginner may make, using only the knowledge of knitting she has already acquired from that and preceding chapters. In short, while the advanced knitter may dip into it wherever she pleases, the beginner should begin this book at the beginning and read it like a novel, practicing each step as she reads.

Through the years, I have learned that the best and quickest way for a beginner to become thoroughly acquainted with all the basics is to learn one stitch at a time, practicing this one stitch until she is proficient enough at working it that she can knit a large expanse of fabric effortlessly and with no errors. The first of these is, of course, the knit stitch. Before going on to the next basic stitch, purl, the beginner should make one or more simple items using only the knit stitch. When the second basic stitch is learned, a few more simple items should be made, using a combination of the knit and the purl stitch.

When the two most basic knitting stitches have been mastered, and several items made from them, the knitter will be able to do these automatically. She can then concentrate on learning the basic increase and decrease called for in many directions. Basic increases and decreases are very simple to do and are needed in instances where a curved neckline or arm opening is desired. From knit, purl, increase and decrease, the knitter will then progress to other basic stitches, techniques and combinations thereof very quickly, for she will have become used to the yarn, knitting needles, and most often-used stitches, and should have no trouble reading and interpreting the simple directions.

Signe Gorman of Canoga Park, California, an accomplished artist, put aside her palettes and charcoal pencils to take knitting needles in hand to learn to knit. As a beginner, she helped in my experiment to determine if a beginning knitter could understand and actually work from the instructions and directions in this book. With no more knowledge of knitting than appears in the first chapter, she knitted the tote bag pictured there without so much as a dropped stitch and without asking a single question, pleased as Punch that knitting was so much fun. She then knitted the tote bag in Stockinette Stitch from Chapter 2, the sleeveless shell and skirt from Chapter 3, the pullover in Chapter 4, and so on through the book, finally knitting the girls' shell and shorts in Chapter 7 and the toga top in Eyelet Lace in Chapter 9. I was thus assured that the content of the book justifies its title.

Bess Braun of Malibu Canyon, a good friend and neighbor, took time from her busy schedule to help knit many of the more advanced items. Again, there were no dropped stitches, no confusion, and no difficulty with the directions, proving that a median knitter will have no trouble working the more intricate patterns in Chapter 8.

Beginning and advanced knitters alike will discover that the classic simplicity of the items in this book will not go out of style with the whims of current fashion. They can be enhanced in an endless variety of ways with many surface decoration ideas, most of which have been designed especially for this book. These appear in Chapters 6 and 7. Many of them are so easy as to be understood with no more effort than examination of the photographs. If a knitter can use scissors and thread a needle, she has within her power the ability to decorate simple hand-knit items in many interesting ways.

I have endeavored to create within these pages, a knitting book which is like no other; one which is at once practical, unique, of interest to both beginning and advanced knitters—and most of all, easy.

Part One

THE BASICS OF KNITTING

Chapter 1

YARNS

For all practical purposes, there are three weights of yarn in general use by the knitter: light, medium, and heavy. The most popular yarns, illustrated above, are shown in actual size, from left to right: lightweight wool, lightweight synthetic fiber, medium-weight knitting worsted (a wool yarn), medium-weight synthetic fiber, heavyweight bulky yarn (usually of wool or a wool-nylon blend), and heavyweight super-bulky yarn (usually of wool).

The lightweight yarns are knitted with #4 through #8 needles, depending on the item being made and the pattern stitch being used. The medium weights generally require needles #7 through #10½, and the heavyweights, #10½ through #15.

The extra-fine yarns, taking very small needles and a great deal of time to work, have fallen into disfavor with knitters in recent years and are not included herein.

KNITTING IMPLEMENTS

Listed below is a group of knitting implements that the knitter should assemble in a convenient place near at hand. With this small collection of knitting needles and accessories, the knitter will have the implements needed for most of the patterns and directions to be found throughout the following pages.

Knitting needles, straight plastic, 10" length; 1 pair each in the following sizes: #5, 6, 7, 8, 9, 10, 10½, 11
Plastic yarn needle
Metal yarn needles in several sizes
Crochet hooks, 1 each of the following sizes: #2, 1, 0, 00, F, and G
Scissors
Metal tape measure

KNITTING NEEDLES

American Sizes:	# 0	1	2	3	4	5	6	7	8	9	10	10½	11	13	15
British Equivalent:	#13	12	11	10	9	8	7	6	5	4	3		2		

HOW TO CAST ON

SLIP LOOP

To begin an item, the following method should be used: Pull out approximately 12" of yarn for every 10 stitches to be cast on. Place this free end to your left and the skein of yarn to your right. Make a slip loop at this point and place it on a knitting needle. See photo below.

CASTING ON TO BEGIN AN ITEM

FIRST STEP

Holding this needle in your right hand and using the free end of the yarn, loop yarn around thumb or forefinger of left hand, insert needle into this loop, and bring skein end of yarn under and over needle.

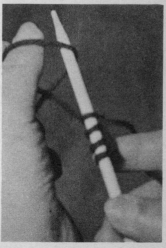

SECOND STEP

Draw this yarn though loop on left hand. Pull free end of yarn to the left to tighten loop on needle. Repeat this procedure until the desired number of loops (including the slip loop first made) has been cast on.

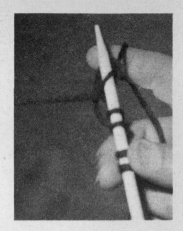

CASTING ON TO AN ITEM ALREADY IN PROGRESS

To cast on stitches at the beginning of a row of knitting already in progress (as for knitted-in sleeves), the following method should be used:

FIRST STEP

Insert right-hand needle into first stitch on left-hand needle, as if to knit; wrap yarn around needle and draw loop through (as in a knit stitch), but do not slip this stitch off left needle.

Instead, slip the loop just made from the right needle onto the left needle, then repeat, inserting right needle into stitch just made, until the desired number of stitches have been added.

THE BASIC KNIT STITCH

The most basic of all knitting, and the stitch beginners always learn first, is the knit stitch. The easiest way to learn it is to remember, when practicing, that it consists of four actions of the needles, and the beginner should at first count these as each stitch is made across the needles. The most common error made in knitting is neglecting to complete action 3, and the partially worked stitch is slipped off the left needle improperly, so that an unwanted extra stitch is added unknowingly, the result of which is a hole in the fabric on the next row. This error is avoided by counting 1, 2, 3, 4 on every stitch at first, which is far less trouble than ripping back, starting over, or (horror of horrors!) completing an item with a mistake in it.

When the beginner practices the 1, 2, 3, 4 procedure given below, she will find that in a very short time an "automatic pilot" in her mind will take over and do the counting for her.

ACTION 1

Insert right needle into stitch (loop) nearest the point of left needle, from front to back, keeping the working yarn at the back.

ACTION 2

Wrap working yarn around point of right needle, from right to left, and from back to front.

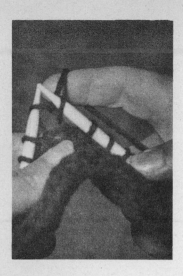

ACTION 3

Draw yarn, with the point of right needle, through loop on left needle.

ACTION 4

Slip left loop just worked off left needle, and slip the loop made well back onto the body of right needle.

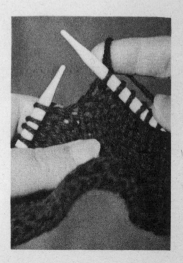

Repeat this procedure on each stitch across the left needle. When this has been done, and all the stitches that were on the left needle have been transferred to the right needle, place the needle holding the stitches in the left hand, the empty needle in the right hand, and begin another row in exactly the same way.

Each time you have knitted all the stitches from one needle to the other, you have worked one row. When counting rows in a specific set of directions, count each back and each front fabric row as a separate row. For example: If directions call for you to "knit 4 rows," you will alternately knit across 2 rows on what is to be the front of the fabric and 2 rows across what will be the back of the fabric. This rule remains the same whether the fabric is reversible or whether the front and reverse sides are different textures.

HOW TO HOLD WORKING YARN

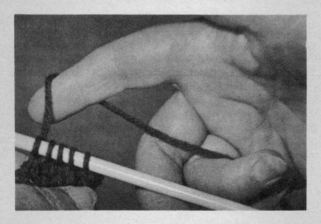

In the photo above, the hand is turned slightly upward in order to illustrate the proper way to hold the working yarn in the right hand. Holding it in this manner while knitting yields a snug, even fabric, with a neat appearance and uniform stitches.

THE GARTER STITCH

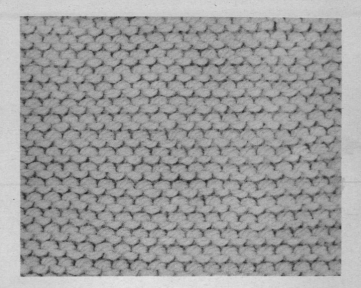

When the basic knit stitch is worked across the stitches on every row, it forms an attractive fabric which is called the Garter Stitch. When you have learned only the basic knit stitch, it is possible to start making attractive items such as blouses, tote bags, and many other things. At the same time, you will be "digesting" the first stitch learned, so that when you learn the next basic stitch you will not have to worry about remembering the first one—you will know it so thoroughly by this time that you will do it without conscious thought.

HOW TO BIND OFF IN TWO STEPS

Knit 2 stitches as usual, then with the point of left needle lift the first stitch over the second stitch and off the point of right needle. Knit another stitch and lift the previously knitted stitch over this one. Repeat this procedure until the desired number of stitches has been bound off.

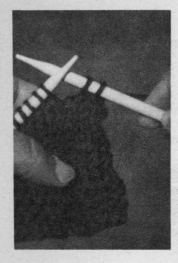

HOW TO SEW A GARTER STITCH SEAM

In the photo below, white yarn has been used to illustrate the method clearly. Seams should be sewn with matching yarn when finishing an item.

ABBREVIATIONS

k	knit
p	purl
st(s)	stitch(es)
o	over (or yarn over)
tog	together
sl	slip
psso	pass slip stitch over knit stitch

You will find only the above abbreviations used throughout this book. For complete clarity, all other words and phrases in connection with knitting actions and techniques are unabbreviated.

STITCH GAUGE

The number of stitches to an inch of fabric sometimes varies from knitter to knitter. This variance is usually due to the fact that there are several methods of holding the working yarn as one is knitting.

At the beginning of most knitting directions, a stitch gauge for the yarn used is given, along with the average knitting-needle size for attaining the specified stitch gauge. Following the needle size, there is usually advice to the knitter to use any size needle required to obtain the proper stitch gauge.

If the stitch gauge varies from the one specified in any given set of directions, the item is likely to turn out ill fitting, either too large or too small. To avoid this, a stitch-gauge swatch should be made, using the specified yarn and needle size, before the item in question is started.

Knit a stitch-gauge swatch by casting on enough stitches so that the swatch will measure 3" or 4" wide if Garter Stitch or Stockinette Stitch is to be used. If another pattern stitch is to be used, particularly a large multiple lacy pattern, cast on enough stitches so that the width of the swatch will be at least 5". Work in the specified pattern until swatch measures about 4" from the beginning. Bind off all stitches loosely. This swatch may be smoothed out either by steam pressing lightly on the reverse side or (if washable) by wetting thoroughly in lukewarm water and drying on a flat surface. This smoothing-out process will generally reveal a more true stitch gauge than when it is left on the needles, unpressed, to be measured.

Using a metal tape measure or ruler, measure the exact number of stitches to 1" of fabric, then measure across a 2" horizontal area to determine if the number of stitches per inch is an average one. If half the number of stitches in the 2" gauge is the same as the 1" gauge, and if this gauge is the correct one for a specific article, then your stitch gauge is probably an average one for the particular type of yarn used.

If a stitch-gauge swatch yields FEWER stitches per inch than are required in a given set of directions, use a SMALL-

ER needle size to obtain the proper number of stitches per inch of fabric. If a stitch-gauge swatch yields MORE stitches per inch than are required, use a LARGER needle size to obtain the proper number of stitches.

Sometimes, in addition to giving a horizontal-stitch gauge, a vertical-row gauge is given. More often than not, this vertical-row gauge is not necessary, inasmuch as most expanses of knitted fabric are measured vertically in inches rather than in rows, and has no real significance in knitting directions except in rare instances where a vertical expanse of fabric is measured in row or pattern units rather than in inches.

BLOCKING

Blocking a knitted item is comparable to pressing the surface and seams of a garment made of woven cloth after it is made and before it is worn. One would not dream of wearing a dress, for example, as it looks when it comes from the sewing machine. It must be pressed carefully to give it a smooth, neat appearance. Blocking a knitted item serves exactly the same purpose.

Blocking an item of simple shape at home is easy and can be done either in separate pieces or after it is assembled. Any item of simple and uncomplicated lines can be blocked in the following manner: Assemble a supply of rustproof pins, a metal tape measure, a supply of terry-cloth towels, and a blocking board.

A blocking board can be a softwood, kitchen cutting board, an old card table into which pins can be pushed, a large piece of framed fiberboard (available at most building supply stores), or any similar board with a large flat surface.

If the item to be blocked is of acrylic or of an unwashable yarn, it should be steamed. This may be done by holding the steam iron about ½" above the reverse side of fabric. Move iron slowly over the entire surface until item is slightly dampened and pliable.

If the item to be blocked is of a washable yarn, wet thoroughly in lukewarm water. Lift out of water using both

15

hands (never pick up wet knitted fabric by an edge or corner), and gently squeeze excess moisture out without wringing or twisting. Roll in a terry-cloth towel and leave for a few minutes so that the absorbent toweling can take up additional moisture. Unroll and remove from towel, again using both hands to lift the wet fabric.

Place the steamed or wet item on the blocking board. Gently smooth out the item to exact desired measurements, using the metal tape measure. If you are blocking a garment, be sure to allow at least an inch or two more than actual body measurements, depending upon how snug or loose fitting you wish the finished garment to be. Pin the item firmly to the blocking board with rustproof pins, placing each pin approximately $1\frac{1}{2}''$ to $2''$ apart. Cover with dry terry-cloth towels and allow item to dry thoroughly, 24 to 36 hours, before removing from board.

BLOCKING AND LAUNDERING MULTICOLOR KNITTED ITEMS

When blocking or laundering knitted items containing more than one color of yarn, it is advisable to use 1 or 2 tablespoonfuls of vinegar in the last rinse water. This will prevent the various colors from running while still damp.

EASY THINGS TO MAKE

COVERED COAT HANGERS

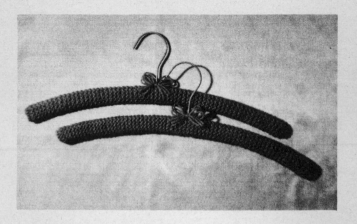

Yarn: Knitting worsted; 1 oz.

Knitting Needles: 1 pair #7 (or any size required to obtain the stitch gauge given below).

Stitch Gauge: 9½ sts equal 2".

Coat Hangers: 2 standard wooden with metal hooks, as shown.

Apply 3 coats of matching or contrasting color nail polish to metal hooks, allowing each coat to dry thoroughly.

Cast on 10 sts and work in Garter Stitch (knit every row) until piece measures 14". Bind off all sts. Fold fabric lengthwise and sew each narrow end tog. Fold in half widthwise and determine exact middle of fold. Insert metal hook through fabric at this point. Stretch sewn ends over coat hanger ends. Sew lengthwise edges tog. Cut 3 strands of matching yarn, each 10" long. Place tog and tie bow at base of hook, as shown.

TOTE BAG IN GARTER STITCH

Size: 12"×13", finished.

Yarn: Heavyweight; super-bulky wool or any similar yarn yielding the proper stitch gauge; 12 oz.

Knitting Needles: 1 pair #11 (or any size required to obtain the stitch gauge given below).

Stitch Gauge: 3 sts equal 1".

Additional Material: Heavy fabric for lining.

NOTE: For decoration suggestions, see Chapter 6 before assembling.

Cast on 35 sts and work in Garter Stitch (knit every row) until piece measures 26". Bind off all sts loosely.

Braided Handle: Cut 15 strands of yarn, each measuring 1½ yards long. Tie a strand of matching yarn around one end, leaving a 2½" tassel. Divide strands into hanks of 5 strands each and make a snug braid measuring 32" long. Tie end as before and clip tassel to 2½".

Assembling and Finishing: Fold bag and sew side seams. Sew tassel ends of braided handle to upper edges of seams, as shown.

CAP-SLEEVE BLOUSE IN GARTER STITCH STRIPE

Size: Directions are given first for bust measurement 32"–34". Changes for larger sizes (36"–38", 40"–42") follow in parentheses. It is suggested that the proper size be circled lightly in pencil throughout directions before beginning.

Yarn: Medium-weight; knitting worsted or any similar yarn yielding the proper stitch gauge; 12 oz white and 2 oz contrasting color.

Knitting Needles: 1 pair #8 (or any size required to obtain the stitch gauge given below).

Stitch Gauge: 9 sts equal 2″; 9 Garter Stitch ridges (18 rows) equal 2″.

Additional Material: Iron-on tape for neckline (optional).

Back and Front are identical. **Make 2 of the following:** Using white, cast on 99 sts and knit across 4 rows. *Drop white, attach contrasting color with a firm double knot and knit across 2 rows. Cut contrasting color and tie end to first contrasting color strand; pick up white and knit across 12 rows*. Repeat between *'s until work measures 17″ (19″, 20½″). When next contrasting color stripe has been completed, knit across next 5 rows (white), and bind off all sts (knitwise) on reverse side loosely.

Collar: Using contrasting color, cast on 6 sts and work in Garter Stitch for 27″. Bind off all sts.

Assembling and Finishing: Trim contrasting color strands to ¾″ on back and front. Place these edges tog and sew shoulder seams, leaving a 10″ opening for neckline. Sew side seams, leaving a 6½″ (7″, 7½″) opening for arms on each side. Using contrasting color, tack collar to back neckline at 2″ intervals. With crochet hook, anchor all loose strands around neckline by pulling these strands through purl sts on reverse side. (When a st is knitted on the front, it automatically forms a purl st on the back.) Place narrow ends of collar tog. Tie a strand of contrasting color yarn tightly around them, 2″ above ends, as shown. Neckline may be backed with iron-on tape, if desired. Block to desired measurements.

Chapter 2

THE BASIC PURL STITCH

As in the basic knit stitch, the basic purl stitch also has 4 distinct actions of the knitting needles that a beginner must learn. The purl stitch is the knit stitch worked backward; that is, when a purl stitch is created, its counterpart, the knit stitch, is automatically formed on the reverse side. When learning the purl stitch, the 4 actions required should also be counted while practicing.

ACTION 1

With working yarn at front, insert right needle into front strand of stitch (loop) nearest the point of left needle, from back to front.

ACTION 2

Wrap working yarn around
point of right needle, from
right to left (the same as
for a knit stitch).

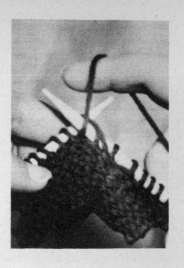

ACTION 3

Draw yarn, with the point
of right needle, through
loop on left needle.

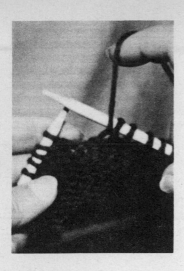

ACTION 4

Slip left loop just worked off left needle. Slip loop just made well back onto the body of right needle.

THE STOCKINETTE STITCH

When the basic knit stitch is worked across the right side and the purl stitch is worked across the reverse side a fabric is created that is called the Stockinette Stitch. In the photos on page 24 the front (or smooth) side of fabric is shown on top. On the bottom is the reverse side.

After you have learned to do the purl stitch well enough so that you do not have to count the four actions on every stitch, practice both the knit and the purl stitches, working across the first row in knit stitches and the next row in purl stitches. Continue alternating knit and purl rows, and soon you will see the Stockinette Stitch taking shape. The knit (right) side will be smooth and the reverse side will be "pearly" or "purly." If you experience any difficulty in distinguishing the right side from the reverse side when starting to practice the Stockinette Stitch, just remember that the purl side looks like an expanse of small pearls (purls), and the knit side looks like a series of smooth, upward-climbing chains (holding the "purls" in place on the reverse side).

When you have learned the purl stitch, and use it in combination with the knit stitch, you now have the knowledge and ability to expand your work to include knitted items in the Stockinette Stitch as well as the Garter Stitch, and a vast number of attractive articles can be made by combining these two fabric textures.

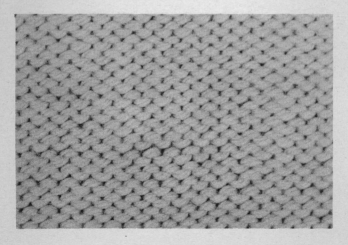

HOW TO SEW A STOCKINETTE STITCH SEAM

RUNNING BACKSTITCH

The quickest and easiest way to seam a knitted item is to use the running backstitch in exactly the same way an article of woven fabric is hand sewn. Pin right sides of fabric edges together, taking care to match stripes or patterns where possible. Work 2 or 3 running stitches along edges, making sure that needle and sewing yarn are penetrating both layers of fabric, then work a backstitch in running stitch just made, as shown.

FLAT STITCH

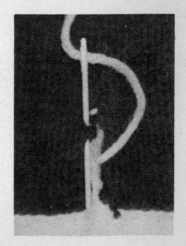

The flat stitch is done with edges of fabric butted together and worked on the right side. This method of sewing a knitted item should only be used on a straight, vertical edge that contains no increases or decreases, and then only if one cares to do it in this manner. Insert yarn needle through 2 vertical strands of the edge stitch of one side, draw sewing yarn up snugly but not too tightly, then insert needle through the corresponding 2 vertical strands on the other fabric edge, as shown. This type of seam can also be used on straight-edged ribbing.

HOW TO SHAPE A NECKLINE
FROM A STRAIGHT EDGE

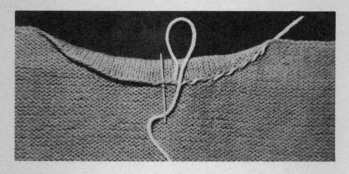

Turn the horizontal upper edge toward the reverse side of the fabric, shaping it into a crescent and making sure that the widest portion, which may vary from ½" to 2", is in the exact middle of the neckline, with curved sides tapering off evenly. Steam press this crescent-shaped curve lightly, or pin to hold. Sew to reverse side of fabric, using the overcast stitch, as shown. This may be done either before or after shoulder seams have been sewn. Matching yarn should always be used.

HOW TO TURN A KNITTED HEM

Sew a hem in a knitted article or garment in exactly the same way a hem of woven cloth is done. Pin hem to desired width and sew to reverse side of fabric, using the overcast stitch, as shown in the photo illustrating how to shape a neckline, above.

HOW TO FINISH A KNITTED EDGE
WITH SINGLE CROCHET

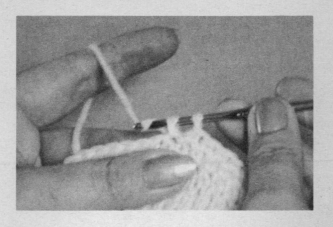

With right side of knitted fabric facing, draw working yarn through the 2 edge strands of knitted fabric at starting point and tie firmly. Insert hook through these same 2 edge strands and draw working yarn through (1 loop on hook), grasp yarn with hook and draw through loop. *Insert hook through next 2 edge strands of knitted fabric (directly to the left) and draw working yarn through; there will now be 2 loops on hook. Grasp working yarn with hook and draw through both of these loops, leaving 1 loop on hook*. Repeat this procedure between *'s for each single crochet, continuing for desired length of knitted-fabric edge. If crocheted edge ends at a corner or angle, break yarn 2" from last single crochet made, draw this end through loop and pull to tighten. If crocheted edge ends at the starting point (first single crochet made), then join these 2 single crochets (first and last made) with a slip stitch, as follows: Insert hook in top of first single crochet made, grasp working yarn with hook, and draw through both strands of single crochet and the loop on hook; break yarn and pull through loop if only 1 row of single crochet is desired. If more than

1 row is needed, do not break yarn after joining with slip stitch, but continue working single crochet stitches in top of each single crochet made on previous row. If crocheted edge does not lie flat, but ruffles along the knitted edge, a smaller crochet hook should be used. If crocheted edge is too tight and causes the knitting to ruffle, a larger crochet hook should be used.

THE CROCHETED CHAIN STITCH

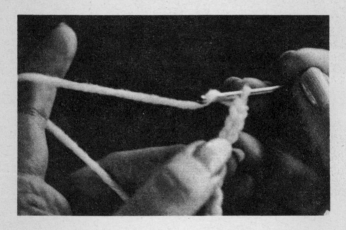

Make a slip loop about 1½" from free end of yarn. Insert crochet hook through loop, catch working yarn with hook and draw through. Again catch working yarn and draw through loop (2 chains made). Continue in this manner, drawing working yarn through each loop made until desired number of chains has been made, or until chain is of the desired length.

EASY THINGS TO MAKE

CAP-SLEEVE BLOUSE IN STOCKINETTE STITCH

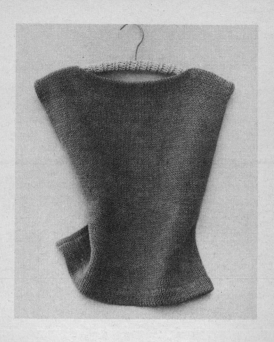

Size: Directions are given first for 32" bust measurement. Changes for larger sizes (34", 36", 38", 40", 42", 44") follow in parentheses. It is suggested that the proper size be circled lightly in pencil throughout directions before beginning.

Yarn: Medium-weight; knitting worsted or any similar yarn yielding the proper stitch gauge; 12 oz.

Knitting Needles: 1 pair #8 (or any size required to obtain the stitch gauge given below).

Stitch Gauge: 9 sts equal 2".

NOTE: Suggestions for decoration may be found in Chapters 6 and 7.

Back and Front are identical. **Make 2 of the following:** Cast on 76 (80, 85, 90, 95, 99, 103) sts and work in Stockinette Stitch until piece measures 21" (21", 22", 22", 22", 23", 23"), or desired length (when measured from shoulder seam to lower edge, plus 1½" hem allowance). Bind off all sts loosely.

Assembling and Finishing: Sew shoulder seams, leaving a 10" opening for neckline. Sew side seams, leaving a 6½" (7", 7", 7½", 7½", 8", 8") opening on each side for arms. Shape a curved neckline at front, pinning to 1½" at widest part of curve. Turn a ⅓" hem at back neckline and around each arm opening. Turn a 1½" hem at lower edge. Block to desired measurements.

PILLOW IN STOCKINETTE STITCH

Size: 14" square.

Yarn: Knitting worsted; 5 oz.

Knitting Needles: One pair #9 (or any size required to obtain the stitch gauge given below).

Stitch Gauge: 8½ sts equal 2".

Crochet Hook: Steel #00.

Additional Material: One 14" square pillow form (available at needlework shops and department store yarn sections).

NOTE: For applied surface decoration, see Chapters 6 and 7.

Make 2 of the following: Cast on 57 sts and work in Stockinette Stitch for 13½". Bind off all sts loosely. Work 2 rows of single crochet around all sides of each piece, working 3 single crochet sts in each corner on each row. Block each piece separately. Using a half strand of yarn, and with reverse side edges tog, sew seams on 3 sides, using over-cast st through inside strands of single crochet sts. Insert pillow form and sew remaining edge of each piece tog.

TOTE BAG IN STOCKINETTE STITCH

Size: 11"×12", finished.

Yarn: Super-bulky wool; 10 oz.

Knitting Needles: One pair #11 (or any size required to obtain the stitch gauge given below).

Stitch Gauge: 6 sts equal 2".

Crochet Hook: Aluminum size G.

Additional Material: Iron-on-fabric backing, 11"×24".

NOTE: See Chapter 7 for surface-weave decoration, which should be applied before pressing on the bonded fabric to reverse side.

Cast on 36 sts and work in Stockinette Stitch until piece measures 26". Bind off all sts loosely. Block piece to 11"×26". Press iron-on fabric to reverse side of knitted piece, leaving 1" on each end free of bonded fabric for hem turn. Sew sides of bag on right side, using flat stitch and a half strand of yarn. Turn down a 1" hem at upper edge and sew with overcast st, using cotton sewing thread.

Handle: Using 3 strands together, crochet a chain 61" long. Tie a single knot in each end. Sew chain to bag, up each side from knotted ends, as shown.

ELBOW-SLEEVE SHIFT IN STOCKINETTE STITCH

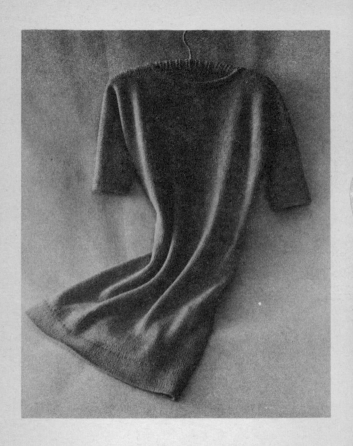

Size: Directions are given first for bust measurement 32"–34". Changes for larger sizes (36"–38", 40"–42") follow in parentheses. It is suggested that the proper size be circled lightly in pencil throughout directions before beginning.

Yarn: Lightweight; sports yarn or any similar yarn yielding the proper stitch gauge; 14 oz.

Knitting Needles: 1 pair #6 (or any size required to obtain the stitch gauge given below).

Stitch Gauge: 11 sts equal 2".

NOTE: For applied surface decoration, see Chapter 6.

Back and Front are identical. **Make 2 of the following:** Beginning at neckline edge, cast on 195 (205, 215) sts and work in Stockinette Stitch for 5" (5½", 6"), then bind off 5 sts at beginning of every row (counting both front and reverse sides as rows) until 95 (105, 115) sts remain. Continue over remaining sts until work is the desired length when measured from shoulder seam to lower edge, plus a 2" hem allowance. Bind off all sts loosely.

Assembling and Finishing: Sew upper sleeve and shoulder seams, leaving a 10" neckline opening. Sew lower sleeve and side seams. Shape a curved neckline at front, shaping widest part of curve to 1½", and hem. Turn a ⅓" hem at back neckline. Turn a 2" hem at lower edge. Block to desired measurements.

CHILD'S COTTON T-SHIRT

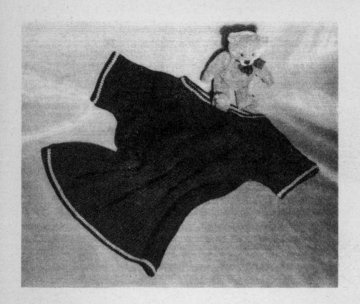

Size: 6-year (24″ chest measurement); 7-year (26″ chest measurement); 8-year (28″ chest measurement). Directions are given first for 6-year size. Changes for larger sizes (7-year, 8-year) follow in parentheses. It is suggested that the proper size be circled lightly in pencil throughout directions before beginning.

Yarn: Lightweight; hand-knitting cotton or any similar yarn yielding the proper stitch gauge; 6 oz main color and 1 oz contrasting color.

Knitting Needles: 1 pair #6 (or any size required to obtain the stitch gauge given below).

Stitch Gauge: 6 sts equal 1″.

Crochet Hook: Steel #2.

Back and Front are identical. **Make 2 of the following:** Cast on 76 (82, 88) sts and work in Stockinette Stitch until piece measures 10" (11", 12"), or desired length from lower edge to underarm. At beginning of next 2 rows, cast on 10 (11, 12) sts (once each side for sleeves) and continue over these 96 (104, 112) sts until sleeve measures 4½" (5", 5½"). Bind off all sts loosely.

Assembling and Finishing: Sew shoulder, sleeve, and side seams, leaving an 8½" opening for neckline. Turn neckline down into a crescent shape at front, with widest part measuring 1½", and sew. Using main color, work 1 row single crochet around neckline, sleeves, and lower edge. Work 2nd and 3rd rows in contrasting color, and work 4th row with main color, as shown. Block to desired measurements.

QUICK-KNIT DECORATOR PILLOW IN STRIPED STOCKINETTE STITCH

Size: 14" square.

Yarn: Super-bulky; 8 oz main color, 4 oz contrasting color.

Knitting Needles: 1 pair #10½ (or any size required to obtain the stitch gauge given below).

Stitch Gauge: 6½ sts equal 2".

Additional Material: One 14" square pillow form (available at needlework shops and department store yarn sections).

Crochet Hook: Aluminum size G.

Make 2 of the following: Using main color, cast on 40 sts and work in Stockinette Stitch for 4 rows. Attach contrasting color and work in Stockinette Stitch for 2 rows. Repeat these alternate stripes until work measures approximately 14″. Complete last stripe if necessary and bind off all sts loosely. Using contrasting color, work 1 row single crochet around all sides of each piece, working 3 single crochet sts in each corner. Block each piece separately. With reverse sides tog, and using a half strand of yarn, sew these 2 edges tog around 3 sides, using overcast st through inside strands of single crochet sts. Insert pillow form and sew remaining edge of each piece tog.

COVERLET

Size: Approximately 42″×60″, exclusive of fringe.

Yarn: Lightweight; sports yarn or any similar yarn yielding the proper stitch gauge; 20 oz.

Knitting Needles: 1 pair #9 (or any size required to obtain the stitch gauge given below).

Stitch Gauge: 9 sts equal 2".

Crochet Hook: Steel #1.

Pattern Stitch: (A multiple of 40 sts).

Row 1: *K 20, bring yarn forward between points of needles, p 20, yarn to back*. Repeat between *'s across row.
Row 2 (and all even-numbered rows): Purl.
Rows 3, 5, 7, 9, 11, 13, 15, 17, and **19:** Same as Row 1.
Row 21: *P 20, yarn to back, k 20, yarn forward*. Repeat between *'s across row.
Rows 23, 25, 27, 29, 31, 33, 35, 37, and **39:** Same as Row 21.
Row 40: Purl.
Repeat from Row 1 for pattern.

Cast on 160 sts and work in pattern stitch until coverlet measures 60". Complete pattern stitch to last-numbered row and bind off all sts loosely.

Finishing: Work 2 rows single crochet around all edges, working 3 single crochets in each corner on each row. Attach fringe as follows: Cut strands, each 4" long. Fold 2 strands in half, pull through a single crochet st, using crochet hook, to form a ½" loop. Pull cut ends through this loop and pull to tighten. Repeat in each single crochet st around coverlet. Steam press lightly on reverse side.

Chapter 3

HOW TO INCREASE

The increase is used to widen an expanse of fabric, giving it a shape other than square or rectangular. This is done by adding (or increasing) stitches in the course of working a row or a series of rows. When directions call for an increase (increase 1 stitch in next stitch) without further instructions as to how to work it, it is done as follows:

Insert right needle into the stitch directly below the next stitch on the left needle and knit it as you would knit a regular stitch, then knit the stitch on the left needle (from which the increase was made) as usual. This is sometimes called a closed increase and is usually called for in directions to widen a garment or other item by one or two stitches at a time.

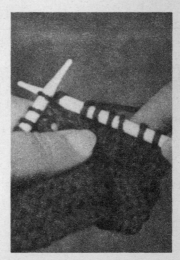

HOW TO DECREASE

The easiest and most common decrease is made by simply knitting or purling two stitches together. When a decrease is called for in a specific set of directions (decrease 1 stitch) without further instructions, the next two stitches are knitted (or purled) together as if they were one stitch. There are other types of decreases used for specific purposes (see Chapter 8), and when they are called for, they are usually accompanied by instructions for working.

THE OPEN INCREASE (OVER)

Most lacy or openwork patterns are based on the open increase, or the "over" or "yarn over," as it is almost universally called, and the decrease distributed throughout a knitted fabric in such a manner as to form a filet or filigree design. The over (o) creates an extra stitch in the next row, with a small round hole or eyelet directly beneath it. These eyelets, spaced in various positions, form the basis of most lacy knitted patterns. The added (over) stitches are always counterbalanced by decreases in direct proportion to the number of overs made on any specific row. The decreases are sometimes done on the same row as the overs and sometimes worked on the next row. This is necessary so that the number of stitches originally cast on will remain the same.

WHEN KNITTING

Work an over
KNIT stitches as fol...
Bring the yarn forward between the points of the
needles (in the same man-
ner as the yarn is brought
forward before working a
purl stitch), then, holding
working yarn in right hand
and over the right needle
toward the back of work,
knit the next stitch from
this rather peculiar work-
ing-yarn position.

WHEN PURLING

Work an over between
PURL stitches as follows:
With yarn in purl position,
wrap it once around the
right needle and bring it
between the points of the
needles, back again to purl
position. Purl the next
stitch or stitches according
to directions.

43

ain color): Work in Stockinette Stitch,
on-numbered rows and purling even-

Rows 11 and 12 (contrasting color): Knit.
Row 13 (main color): Knit.
Row 14 (main color): Purl.
Row 15 and 16 (contrasting color): Knit.
Row 17 (main color): Knit.
Row 18 (main color): Purl.
Row 19 and 20 (contrasting color): Knit.
Repeat from Row 1 for pattern.

Size: Directions are given first for small (bust and hip measurements 32" through 34"). Changes for medium and large (36"–38", 40"–42") follow in parentheses. It is suggested that the proper size be circled lightly in pencil throughout directions before beginning.

Yarn: Medium-weight; knitting worsted, or any similar yarn yielding the proper stitch gauge. Shell, 10 oz white and 2 oz contrasting color. Skirt, 12 oz contrasting color.

Knitting Needles: Shell, 1 pair #8; skirt, 1 pair #9 (or any sizes required to obtain the stitch gauge given below).

Stitch Gauge: Stockinette Stitch on #8, 9 sts equal 2".
Stockinette Stitch on #9, 8½ sts equal 2".

Crochet Hook: Steel #00.

Elastic: Sufficient length for skirt waistband, ¾" width.

Back and front are identical for both shell and skirt.

SLEEVELESS SHELL IN CANDY-STRIPE PATTERN WITH MATCHING SKIRT

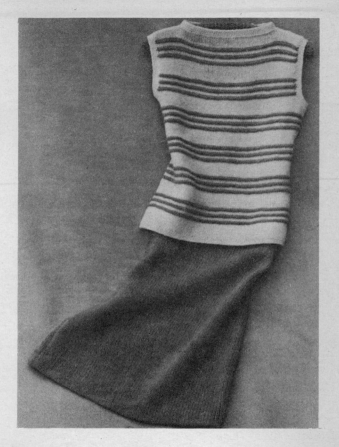

Make 2 each of the following:

SHELL: Using #8 needles and white, cast on 86 (95, 104) sts and work in Candy-Stripe pattern for 12″ (13″, 13½″). At beginning of next 2 rows, bind off 6 sts (once each side) for arm openings, then k 2 tog at beginning and end of a right-side row 2 (3, 4) times. Continue in pattern over remaining sts until arm openings measure 7" (7½", 8"). Bind off all sts loosely.

Assembling and Finishing: Using a half strand of yarn, sew shoulder seams with right sides tog, using running backstitch, and leaving a 9½" opening for neckline. Sew side seams, using flat seam stitch, and taking care to match stripes. Work 4 rows single crochet around arm openings and neckline, and 3 rows single crochet around lower edge.

SKIRT: Using contrasting color and #9 needles, cast on 60 (70, 80) sts and work in Stockinette Stitch for 1½". Increase 1 st each side of a right-side row every inch until there are 70 (80, 90) sts on needles, then increase 1 st each side of a right-side row every 2" until there are 80 (90, 100) sts on needles. Continue without further increases until work measures the desired skirt length from waistline to lower edge, plus 3" additional allowance for waistband and hem.

Assembling and Finishing: Using a half strand of yarn, sew side seams with right sides tog, using running backstitch. Turn a ¾" hem at waistline and sew with overcast stitch, leaving a 1" opening for insertion of elastic. Run elastic through this upper hem and fasten ends securely. Sew the 1" opening. Hem at lower edge to desired skirt length.
Block shell and skirt to desired measurements.

LACY MUFFLER

Yarn: Lightweight; sports yarn or any similar yarn yielding the proper stitch gauge; 3 oz.

Knitting Needles: 1 pair #7 (or any size required to obtain the stitch gauge given below).

Stitch Gauge: 10 sts equal 2".

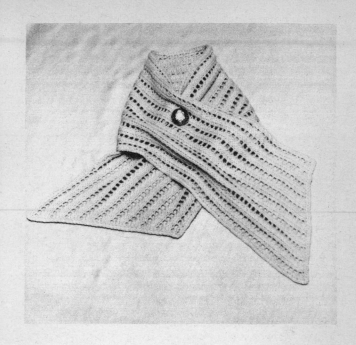

Crochet Hook: Steel #1.

Pattern Stitch: (Multiple of 4 sts plus 1).

Row 1: K 2, *o, k 1, k 2 tog, k 1*. Repeat between *'s across row, ending last repeat: k 2 tog.
Row 2: Purl.

Cast on 41 sts and purl across first row, then repeat pattern st Rows 1 and 2 until muffler measures 36" from start. Complete pattern through Row 2 and bind off all sts loosely. Work 2 rows single crochet around all edges, working 3 single crochet sts in each corner on each row. Block or steam press lightly on reverse side.

Chapter 4

HOW TO KNIT A RIBBED FABRIC

A ribbed fabric is often used when knitting cardigans, pullovers, and other items. It is simply a combination of both knit and purl stitches across a single row, worked alternately or two at a time.

SINGLE RIBBING

The single ribbing pictured above is worked by casting on an even number of stitches and alternating 1 knit stitch and 1 purl stitch, as follows: *K 1 (knit 1 stitch), then bring yarn to the front of work (toward you) between the points of the needles and p 1 (purl 1 stitch), take the yarn to the back of work*. Repeat this procedure between *'s, alternating the knit and purl stitches across the entire row. The needle containing the stitches is now placed in the left hand, and the procedure is repeated until the desired width of ribbing is completed.

DOUBLE RIBBING

Double ribbing is done substantially the same as single ribbing, except that the number of stitches to be cast on must be divisible by 4. *K 2, bring yarn forward between points of needles to front of work, p 2, take yarn to back of work between points of needles*. Repeat this procedure between *'s on every row.

HOW TO PICK UP STITCHES ALONG A KNITTED EDGE

When directions call for stitches to be picked up along a straight vertical edge where no shaping, increasing, or decreasing has been done, simply insert point of needle through the outside strand of each stitch along the edge, as shown. Stitches along horizontal cast-on and bound-off edges can be picked up in the same way.

When directions call for stitches to be picked up along an edge that has been shaped, or where increases or decreases have been made, the following method can be used: Attach yarn to the outside strand of first edge stitch, insert left needle into this stitch and, using right needle and attached working yarn, knit this stitch in the usual way onto right needle. Insert left needle into outside strand of next edge stitch and, using working yarn, knit this stitch onto right needle. Continue in this manner along edge until required number of stitches has been picked up.

Stitches are sometimes picked up on the right side of the fabric and sometimes on the reverse side. Specific directions usually state which side stitches are to be picked up on, depending on the nature of the article being made or the pattern stitch to be used. As a general rule, when directions call for stitches to be picked up, and it is not stated which side of the fabric they are to be picked up on, pick up stitches by the single-needle method on the reverse side of fabric. When the two-needle method is used, pick up stitches on the right side of the fabric.

THE LIFT INCREASE

The lift increase is a semiopen increase used to add stitches to shape an article and is worked as follows: Insert point of left needle (from front to back) into the strand of yarn running between stitches, then knit or purl this extra stitch according to specific directions. As a general rule, when no specific instructions are given other than "lift increase," this extra stitch should be knitted on the right side of the fabric and purled on the reverse side of the fabric.

EASY THINGS TO MAKE FOR FUN AND PRACTICAL USE

SLIPPERS

Size: Women's shoe sizes 6–6½, 7–7½, 8–8½. Directions are given first for size 6–6½. Changes for larger sizes (7–7½, 8–8½) follow in parentheses. For men's slippers, see note in directions on page 52.

Yarn: Super-bulky-type wool or wool-nylon blend; 8 oz.

Knitting Needles: One pair #10½ (or any size required to obtain the stitch gauge given below).

Stitch Gauge: Unblocked ribbing, 4 sts equal 1".

Right and Left slippers are identical. **Make 2 of the following:** Cast on 30 sts and work in k 1, p 1 ribbing for 8" (9", 10"). Do not bind off. NOTE: For men's slippers, omit bows and work 1" additional for each full size beyond 8–8½. For example, if a size 9 or 9½ is required, work ribbing until fabric measures 11"; if size 10–10½ is required, work to 12", etc.

Assembling and Finishing: Thread a yarn needle with a half strand of yarn about 12" long. Thread sts onto this strand from knitting needle, pull tightly to form a closed circle and fasten securely on what is to be the reverse side. Sew a flat seam to 3" above toe, using the flat stitch on right side. Turn toe of slipper inside out and fold heel end of slipper with right sides tog. Using half strand of yarn, sew heel tog with loose overcast st, then pull strand snugly to round heel at folded end. Fasten securely.

Bows: Cast on 8 sts and knit across 2 rows, then work in Stockinette Stitch until piece measures 2½" from start. With reverse side facing, knit across next 2 rows and bind off all sts knitwise on reverse side. Wrap a half strand of yarn around middle of bow 3 times and tie tightly on reverse side. Tack bow to toe, as shown.

GOLF CLUB COVERS

Size: Directions are given first for irons. Changes for woods follow in parentheses.

Yarn: Knitting worsted; about ¾ oz for each cover.

Knitting Needles: For irons, use 1 pair #6 (or any size required to obtain stitch gauge given below). For woods, use 1 pair #8 (or any size required to obtain stitch gauge given on page 53).

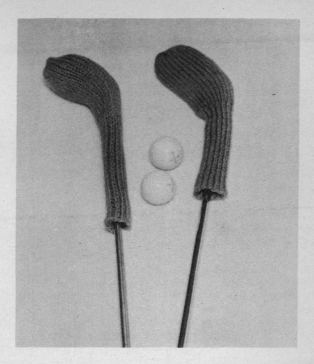

Stitch Gauge: Stockinette Stitch on #6 needles, 10 sts equal 2".
Stockinette Stitch on #8 needles, 9 sts equal 2".

Cast on 26 (28) sts and work in k 1, p 1 ribbing for 4½", then work in Stockinette Stitch for 3½" (4½"). Work next right-side row as follows: k 2 tog on each 2 sts across row. Do not bind off. Cut working yarn about 18" from fabric. Thread this through a yarn needle and slip sts from knitting needle onto cut strand. Pull these sts into a closed circle and fasten securely on reverse side. Sew vertical edges tog from closed circle to lower ribbed edge. Block or steam press lightly on reverse side.

CHILD'S PULLOVER

Size: 2–3 years (22″ chest measurement); 4–5 years (24″ chest measurement). Directions are given first for smaller size; changes for larger size follow in parentheses.

Yarn: Knitting worsted; 8 oz.

Knitting Needles: For size 2–3, use 1 pair #8; for size 4–5, use 1 pair #9 (or any size required to obtain the proper stitch gauge given below).

Stitch Gauge: Stockinette Stitch on #8 needles, 9 sts equal 2″.
Stockinette Stitch on #9 needles, 8½ sts equal 2″.

Crochet Hook: Steel #00.

Back and Front are identical. **Make 2 of the following:** Cast on 59 sts and work in Stockinette Stitch for 7″, or desired length from lower edge to underarm. Shape sleeves:

54

At the beginning of next 4 rows, cast on 12 sts. There will now be 24 sts added on each side. Continue over these 107 sts until sleeves measure 4½" (5½") when measured straight up from underarm, then bind off 12 sts at beginning of next 4 rows. On next row, bind off all remaining sts loosely.

CUFFS: Sew shoulders and upper edges of sleeve seams, leaving an 8½" opening for neckline. With reverse side facing, pick up 26 sts along lower edge of sleeve. Work in k 1, p 1 ribbing for 2". Bind off all sts very loosely, knitting the knit sts and purling the purl sts. Repeat along corresponding cuff edge on opposite sleeve.

Assembling and Finishing: Sew lower sleeve and side seams. Work 3 rows single crochet around neck and lower edge. Block to desired measurements.

CHILD'S CAP

Size: Fits head sizes 2 through 6 years.

Yarn: Knitting worsted; 4 oz.

Knitting Needles: 1 pair #8 (or any size required to obtain the stitch gauge given below).

Stitch Gauge: Blocked ribbing swatch, 9 sts equal 2".

Cast on 84 sts and work in k 2, p 2 ribbing until cap measures 9" from start. NOTE: Cap to match Child's Pullover, on page 54, can be worked in k 1, p 1 ribbing.

Assembling: Do not bind off. Cut yarn 18" from work, thread cut end through yarn needle and slip sts from knitting needle onto this strand. Draw up strand so that stitches form a tight closed circle. Fasten securely and sew side edges of cap from the closed circle to lower edge.

MITTENS

Size: Small (child's size 6–8 years); medium (women's); large (men's). Directions are given first for small. Changes for larger sizes (medium, large) follow in parentheses.

Yarn: Knitting worsted; 3oz.

Knitting Needles: 1 pair #6 for ribbing and 1 pair #8 (or any size required to obtain stitch gauge given below).

Stitch Gauge: Stockinette Stitch on #8 needles, 4½ sts equal 1″.

Right- and Left-hand mittens are reversible and identical. **Make 2 of the following:** Using #6 needles, cast on 30 (34, 38) sts and work in k 1, p 1 ribbing for 1¾″ (2″, 2″). Change to #8 needles and work in Stockinette Stitch for 2 rows. Shape thumb: With right side facing, k 14 (16, 18), lift increase, k 2, lift increase, knit to end of row. Purl

57

across reverse side. Next row: Knit across to st directly above first lift increase, lift increase, knit across to st directly above second lift increase, k 1, lift increase, knit to end of row. Next row: Purl. Repeat these last 2 rows until there are 12 (14, 16) sts between lift increases, then work in Stockinette Stitch without further increases until work measures 3¾ (5", 5½") from start.

Shape hand: On next right-side row, knit across 14 (16, 18) sts; turn work and purl back. Work in Stockinette Stitch over these 14 (16, 18) sts until piece measures 2¾" (3½", 4") from separation, then k 2 tog at beginning and end of each right-side row until 8 (10, 12) sts remain. Bind off on next right-side row. Tie yarn to back of first st on thumb piece and knit across 12 (14, 16) sts. Turn work and purl back. Work in Stockinette Stitch over these 12 (14, 16) sts until piece measures 1½" (1¾", 2") from separation, then k 2 tog at begining and end of each right-side row until 8 (10, 12) sts remain. Bind off on next right-side row. Tie yarn to back of first st of remaining sts and complete as for first hand piece.

Assembling: Sew cuff, hand piece, and thumb seams with right sides tog, using running backstitch and half strand of yarn. Block to desired measurements or steam press lightly on reverse side.

SLEEVELESS PULLOVER

Size: Directions are given first for 40" chest measurement. Changes for larger sizes (42", 44") follow in parentheses.

Yarn: Knitting worsted; 10 oz main color, 2 oz contrasting color.

Knitting Needles: 1 pair #6 for ribbed collar and 1 pair #8 (or any size required to obtain stitch gauge given below).

Stitch Gauge: Stockinette Stitch on #8 needles, 9 sts equal 2".

Crochet Hook: Steel #00.

NOTE: If a larger or smaller size is needed, it is suggested that materials be purchased in a department store or knit shop employing a knitting instructor, so that directions and assistance can be obtained for sizes not given.

BACK: Using main color and #8 needles, cast on 90 (94, 98) sts and work in k 1, p 1 ribbing for 2½". Then change colors for stripes as follows: Break main color, attach contrasting color; work in Stockinette Stitch for 4 rows Break contrasting color, attach main color; work in Stockinette Stitch for 8 rows. Repeat until work measures 16" (16" 16½"). Shape arm openings: Continuing in striped pattern, bind off 6 sts at beginning of next 2 rows (once each side), then k 2 tog at beginning and end of each right-side row 4 times. Continue over these 70 (74, 78) sts until arm openings measure 8½" (8½", 9"). At beginning of next right-side row, bind off 22 (23, 24) sts, knit across 26 (28, 30) sts (counting st on right needle), and bind off remaining 22 (23, 24) sts. Break yarn. Attach main color and using #6 needles, work in k 1, p 1 ribbing over these middle 26 (28, 30) sts for 5". Bind off all sts very loosely, knitting the knit sts and purling the purl sts.

FRONT: Work as for back until arm openings measure 6½" (6½", 7"). Shape neckline: With right side facing, k 26 (28, 30), bind off 18 sts, knit to end of row. Working each shoulder separately, k 2 tog on a right-side row at neckline edge only until 22 (23, 24) sts remain. When arm openings measure 8½" (8½", 9"), bind off all sts loosely. Attach yarn at neck edge of corresponding shoulder and work the same.

FRONT COLLAR: Using #6 needles and main color, cast on 52 (52, 54) sts and work in k 1, p 1 ribbing until piece measures 5". Bind off all sts very loosely, knitting the knit sts and purling the purl sts.

Assembling and Finishing: Sew front collar to front neckline at cast-on edge. Sew shoulder and collar seams, taking care to sew ribbing so that right side of seam will show when collar is turned down. Sew side seams. Using main color, work 2 rows of single crochet around arm openings. Block to desired measurements.

SHORT-SLEEVE BLOUSE WITH GARTER TRIM

Size: Directions are given for size 30"–32" bust measurement. Changes for larger sizes (34"–36", 38"–40", 42"–44") follow in parentheses. It is suggested that the proper size be circled lightly in pencil throughout directions before beginning.

Yarn: Medium-weight; knitting worsted or any similar yarn yielding the proper stitch gauge; 12 oz.

Knitting Needles: 1 pair #8 (or any size required to obtain the stitch gauge given below).

Stitch Gauge: 9 sts equal 2".

Front and Back are identical. **Make 2 of the following:** Cast on 71 (81, 91, 101) sts and knit across 4 rows, then (begining with a knit row) work in Stockinette Stitch until piece measures 14" (14", 15", 15") from start. Shape sleeves: At beginning of next 2 rows, cast on 10 sts (once each side). When sleeves measure 6" (6½, 7", 7½"), and beginning on next reverse-side row, knit across 4 rows and bind off all sts (knitwise) on reverse side loosely.

Sleeve Edging: Sew shoulder seams on reverse side, using overcast st and leaving a 9½" (9½", 10", 10") opening for neckline, as shown. With reverse side facing, pick up 47 (50, 53, 56) sts along sleeve edge. Knit across 5 rows and bind off all sts (knitwise) on reverse side loosely.

Assembling: Sew underarm and side seams. See Chapters 6 and 7 for decorative suggestions. Block to desired measurements.

PULLOVER

Size: Directions are given first for size 38"–40" bust, or chest, measurement. Changes for larger size (42"–44") follow in parentheses.

Yarn: Knitting worsted; 20 oz.

Knitting Needles: 1 pair #7 for ribbing (both sizes) and 1 pair #9, 14" length, for size 38"–40" (or any size required to obtain the stitch gauge given below), or 1 pair #10, 14" length, for size 42"–44" (or any size required to obtain the stitch gauge given below).

Stitch Gauge: Stockinette Stitch on #9 needles, 8½ sts equal 2".
Stockinette Stitch on #10 needles, 8 sts equal 2".

Back and Front are identical. **Make 2 of the following:** Using #7 needles, cast on 90 sts and work in k 1, p 1

ribbing for 2½". Change to larger size needles and work in Stockinette Stitch until piece measures 14½" (15½") from start. Shape sleeves: At beginning of next 10 rows (counting both right and reverse sides as rows), cast on 10 sts. Continue over these 190 sts until sleeve measures 8½" (9½") when measured straight up from underarm to upper edge. Bind off all sts very loosely.

Use half strand of yarn for all sewing.

Ribbed Cuffs: Sew ½" seams in shoulders and upper sleeves, using running backstitch on reverse side and leaving a 9" opening in the middle for neckline. With reverse side facing and using #7 needle, pick up 44 (48) sts along lower edge of sleeve. Work in k 1, p 1 ribbing for 3½" (or until sleeve is the desired length from underarm to lower edge). Bind off all sts very loosely, knitting the knit sts and purling the purl sts.

Assembling and Finishing: Sew underarm and side seams. Turn front neckline down into a crescent shape, with widest part measuring 1½", and sew with overcast st. Turn back neckline down ½" and sew. Block to desired measurements.

BABY JACKET

Size: 3 to 6 months.

Yarn: Lightweight; sports or baby yarn in white or desired color; 4 oz.

Knitting Needles: 1 pair #6 (or any size required to obtain the stitch gauge given below).

Stitch Gauge: 11 sts equal 2".

Additional Material: Approximately 22" satin ribbon, ¼" wide.

BACK: Cast on 60 sts and knit across 4 rows, then (beginning with a knit row) work in Stockinette Stitch until piece measures 7". Sleeve insets: At beginning of the next 2 rows, bind off 9 sts. When sleeve insets measure 3½", bind off all sts loosely.

LEFT FRONT: Cast on 30 sts and knit across 4 rows, then (beginning with a knit row) work in Stockinette Stitch until piece measures 7". Sleeve inset: At beginning of next right-side row, bind off 9 sts. Continue until sleeve inset measures 1½". Shape neckline: At beginning of next reverse-side row, bind off 4 sts, then p 2 tog at beginning of a reverse-side row (neckline edge) until 14 sts remain. When sleeve inset measures 3½", bind off all sts loosely.

RIGHT FRONT: Work as for left front until piece measures 7". Sleeve inset: At beginning of next reverse-side row, bind off 9 sts. Continue until sleeve inset measures 1½". Shape neckline: At beginning of next right-side row, bind off 4 sts, then k 2 tog at beginning of right-side row (neckline edge) until 14 sts remain. When sleeve inset meaasures 3½", bind off all sts loosely.

SLEEVES: Cast on 38 sts and work in Stockinette Stitch for 2", then k 2 tog at beginning and end of a right-side row every ¾" until 26 sts remain. When sleeve measures 7" (and beginning on a reverse-side row), knit across 4 rows and bind off all sts (knitwise) on reverse side loosely.

NECKBAND: Sew shoulder seams. With right side facing, pick up 46 sts around neckline. Knit across 4 rows. Bind off all sts (knitwise) on reverse side loosely.

CENTER FRONT BANDS: With right side facing, pick up 42 sts along center front edge. Complete as for neckband. Repeat on corresponding center front edge.

Assembling and Finishing: Sew side seams. Set sleeves into insets by sewing cast-on sts of sleeves to straight edges across shoulders. Sew upper vertical edges of sleeves to underarm bound-off sts of insets. Sew remainder of vertical sleeve edges tog from underarm to Garter Stitch band at lower edge. Block to desired measurements. Thread ribbon through stitches at base of neckband and tie ends into a bow, as shown.

REVERSIBLE TWEED PATTERN

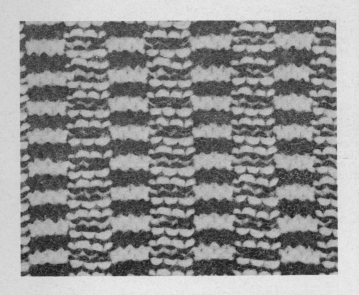

Using color A, cast on a multiple of 6 stitches plus 3.

Row 1: (Color A) K 3, *p 3, k 3*. Repeat between *'s across row.
Row 2: (Color A) Same as Row 1.
Row 3: (Color B) Same as Row 1.
Row 4: (Color B) Same as Row 1.

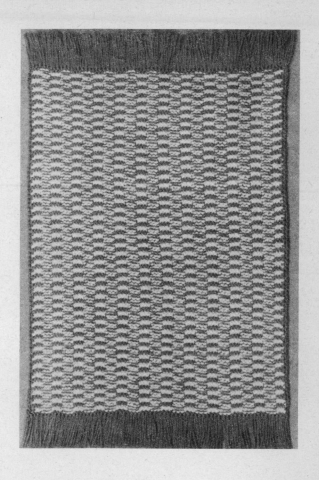

Size: 21"×29", exclusive of fringe.

Yarn: Knitting worsted; 12 oz Color A, 8 oz Color B.

Knitting Needles: 1 pair #10½ (or any size required to obtain the stitch gauge given below).

Stitch Gauge: Pattern stitch, using yarn double strand, 7 sts equal 2".

Crochet Hook: Aluminum size F.

Using yarn double strand throughout, cast on 69 sts in Color A. Work in Reversible Tweed pattern, changing colors as indicated, until piece measures 28½". Complete pattern in Color A through Row 2 and bind off all sts loosely.

Finishing: Using Color A double strand, work 1 row single crochet along each lengthwise side of fabric.

Fringe: Using Color A, cut strands, each measuring 4" long. Holding 2 strands tog, fold in half. Using crochet hook, pull folded end through first st along crosswise edge to form a ¾" loop. Pull cut ends through this loop and pull to tighten. Repeat on each st along both crosswise edges, as shown. Block to exact size.

Chapter 5

KNITTED BUTTONHOLES, THE QUICK, NEAT, AND EASY WAY

Knitted buttonholes along the front of a cardigan or other garment can be made easily and neatly on a Garter Stitch fabric base, throughout which are evenly spaced overs. This strip can either be knitted by picking up stitches along the front of a cardigan, or it can be done separately and sewn on when the garment is completed. See illustration on page 74.

CROCHETED BUTTONHOLES ON A KNITTED EDGE

Crocheted buttonholes are neat and easy, and can be made quickly. Most directions calling for knitted buttonhole bands worked separately from the garment can be substituted with crocheted bands, if desired. See illustration on page 72.

In Chapter 2, directions were given for finishing a knitted edge with single crochet. Working buttonholes in crochet is simply an extension of this, and if you have already learned how to do a finished edge of crochet, working crocheted buttonholes will be quickly and easily learned.

Work as many rows of single crochet as desired along the knitted edge on which the buttonhole band is to be made, or as many as are called for in any specific set of directions. Two or three rows of single crochet are usually worked before the buttonhole rows are done.

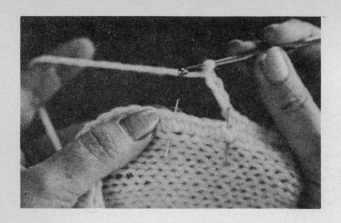

On the first buttonhole row, work as follows: Measure buttons to be used to determine their diameter in inches or fractions thereof; determine how many buttons are to be used and where they will be placed.

NOTE: Work buttonholes on the right front edge of women's wear and on the left front edge of men's wear.

Mark the place where each buttonhole is to be worked by placing 2 straight pins at these points, leaving a space between each pair of pins that is the exact diameter of the buttons to be used. Work a single crochet in the top of each single crochet made on previous row until a pair of pins is reached; then make a crochet chain the exact length of the space between pins. To make a crochet chain, insert crochet hook through loop, catch working yarn with hook and draw through. Continue in this manner, drawing working yarn through each loop formed, until desired number of chains has been made. Single crochet in next stitch directly to the left of second pin and in each stitch thereafter until the next pair of pins is reached. Pins can be removed after each buttonhole chain is worked. Continue

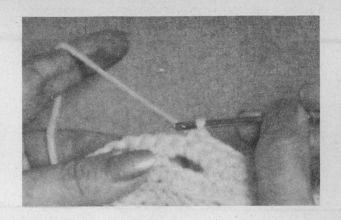

this procedure until all buttonholes have been made and end of row has been reached.

On second buttonhole row, work a single crochet in the top of each single crochet made on previous row until a buttonhole is reached. Work as many single crochet stitches through this chain as were skipped on the previous row. For example, if button width (between pins) spanned 3 single crochet stitches, then work 3 single crochet stitches through the buttonhole chain. Continue in this manner until row has been completed, then work as many single crochet rows over the last buttonhole row as desired. Buttonhole band and corresponding button band, which should contain as many rows of single crochet as the buttonhole band, should be at least 1″ in width.

CARDIGAN BLOUSE WITH CROCHETED BUTTONHOLES AND SHORT KNITTED-IN SLEEVES

Size: Directions are given first for bust size 32″–34″. Changes for larger sizes (36″–38″, 40″–42″) follow in parentheses.

Yarn: Medium-weight; knitting worsted or any similar yarn yielding the proper stitch gauge; 14 oz.

Knitting Needles: 1 pair #8 (or any size required to obtain the stitch gauge given below).

Stitch Gauge: 9 sts equal 2".

Crochet Hook: Steel #00.

Buttons: 5 of desired size. For 1/2" or 3/4" matching yarn buttons, see instructions on pages 77–78.

BACK: Cast on 76 (84, 92) sts and work in Stockinette Stitch for 14" or desired length from lower edge to underarm. Shape sleeves: At beginning of next 2 rows (once each side), cast on 10 sts. Continue over these 96 (104, 112) sts until sleeves measure 7" (7 1/2", 8") when measured straight up from underarm to upper edge. Bind off all sts very loosely.

LEFT FRONT: Cast on 38 (42, 46) sts and work in Stockinette Stitch for 14", or desired length from lower edge to underarm. Shape left sleeve: At beginning of next right-side row, cast on 10 sts. Continue over these 48 (52, 56) sts until sleeve measures 3 3/4" (4", 4 1/2"). Shape neckline: At beginning of next reverse-side row, bind off 7 (8, 9) sts, then k 2 tog at neckline edge only, on every right-side row, 3 times. Continue working without further decreases until sleeve measures 7" (7 1/2", 8"). Bind off all sts very loosely.

RIGHT FRONT: Work as for left front, except: cast on for right sleeve at beginning of reverse-side row, and bind off for neckline at beginning of right-side row.

Assembling and Finishing: Using a half strand of yarn, sew upper sleeve and shoulder seams. Sew underside of sleeve and side seams. Beginning at center back of neckline, work 5 rows of single crochet around entire outside edges, working 3 single crochet in each corner on each row, and working 5 buttonholes, evenly spaced, along right-front edge on 3rd and 4th rows. Beginning at underarm seam, work 5 rows of single crochet around each sleeve edge. Sew buttons on left-front crocheted edge to correspond with buttonholes.

73

CARDIGAN WITH KNITTED BUTTONHOLES AND KNITTED-IN SLEEVES

Size: Directions are given first for bust or chest measurement 30″–32″. Changes for larger sizes (34″–36″, 38″–40″) follow in parentheses. It is suggested that the proper size be circled lightly in pencil throughout directions before beginning.

Yarn: Knitting worsted; 20 oz.

Knitting Needles: 1 pair #6 for ribbed cuffs (all sizes) and:

1 pair #7 for size 30"–32"
1 pair #8 for size 34"–36" } 14" length
1 pair #9 for size 38"–40"

or any size required to obtain the proper stitch gauge given below.

Stitch Gauge: Stockinette Stitch on #7 needles, 9½ sts equal 2".

Stockinette Stitch on #8 needles, 9 sts equal 2".

Stockinette Stitch on #9 needles, 8½ sts equal 2".

Buttons: 6, each ½" diameter. For ½" matching yarn buttons, see instructions on page 77.

BACK: Using larger size needles, cast on 90 sts and work in Stockinette Stitch for 1½", then knit (one row only) across the purl side of fabric for hemline turn. Continue in Stockinette Stitch until work measures 13" (14", 15") from hemline-turn row. Shape sleeves: At beginning of next 10 rows (counting both right and reverse sides as rows), cast on 10 sts, then continue over these 190 sts until sleeves measure 7" (7½", 8") when measured straight up from underarm to upper edge. Bind off all sts very loosely.

LEFT FRONT: Using larger needles, cast on 44 sts and work as for back to underarm. Shape left sleeve: Cast on 10 sts at beginning of every right-side row 5 times. Continue working over these 94 sts until sleeve measures 2½" (3", 3½"). Shape neckline: K 2 tog at neckline edge (opposite side from sleeve) on every right-side row until 80 sts remain. When sleeve measures 7" (7½", 8"), bind off all sts very loosely.

RIGHT FRONT: Work as for left front, except: cast on sts for right sleeve with reverse side facing (opposite side to left sleeve), then complete as for left front.

Use half strand of yarn for all sewing.

RIBBED CUFFS: Sew shoulder and upper sleeve seams on reverse side with running backstitch. Using #6 needles, and with right side facing, pick up 40 (44, 50) sts along lower edge of sleeve. Work in k 1, p 1 ribbing for 3½" (or until sleeve is desired length from underarm to lower edge). Bind off all sts very loosely, knitting the knit sts and purling the purl sts.

Sew underarm and side seams.

BUTTONHOLE BAND: Using larger needles, pick up 90 (94, 96) sts between center back of neckline and lower edge to hemline-turn row only. Do not pick up sts along the edge of this hemline-turn portion.

NOTE: For men's and boy's cardigans, pick up these sts along left-center front edge, and knit across 6 rows. For women's and girls' cardigans, pick up these sts along right-center front edge, and knit across 5 rows.

Next row: With reverse side facing, place a pin at first neckline decrease. Beginning at center back neckline, knit to pin, o (remove pin), and *k 9 (k 9, k 10), o*. Repeat instructions for proper size between *'s 5 times, knit to end of row. There will now be a total of 6 overs, which serve as buttonholes and will accommodate ½" buttons. Next row: *K to o, k 2 tog*. Repeat between *'s until last o has been reached and worked; knit to end of row.

Knit across next 4 rows, then bind off all sts (knitwise) on reverse side very loosely.

BUTTON BAND: Using larger needles, pick up 90 (94, 96) sts on opposite side, between center back of neckline and lower edge, omitting edge of hemline-turn portion, as on opposite side. Knit across 11 rows, then bind off all sts (knit-wise) on reverse side very loosely.

Assembling and Finishing: Sew narrow edges of button bands tog at back neckline. At lower edge, turn hem at purl-ridge row and sew to reverse side, using overcast st. Sew buttons on button band to correspond to buttonholes. Block to desired measurements.

QUICK AND EASY MATCHING YARN BUTTONS

See illustration on page 72.

BUTTONS, ½" DIAMETER

Using a #1 steel crochet hook and ½" diameter plastic rings, work 14 single crochet sts through ring. Slip st into first single crochet worked, then work a single crochet st in each single crochet st of first round. Slip st, as in first round. Cut yarn about 12" from button, draw through loop and pull to tighten. Thread cut yarn through yarn needle. Using overcast st, run yarn needle through every other edge st, turn cup-shaped edge downward to back of ring, and pull yarn into a tight closed circle. Fasten securely, insert yarn needle through button base, draw yarn end through and clip close to sts. Sew to garment through this closed-circle shank.

BUTTONS, ¾" DIAMETER

Using a #00 steel crochet hook and a ½" plastic ring, work 12 single crochet sts through ring. Slip st into first single crochet worked, then work 12 single crochet sts again through ring, over the first round of sts. Slip st, as in first round; cut yarn, draw through loop and pull to tighten. With crochet hook, pull cut end through sts on reverse side and trim close to sts. Sew to garment with matching yarn, inserting yarn needle up through a st at ring center, then down through a st directly opposite. Fasten ends of sewing yarn on reverse side by tying a firm double knot and clipping ends 1/2" from fabric.

Part Two

DECORATIVE MOTIFS

Chapter 6

YARNCRAFT FLOWERS AND LEAVES

GENERAL DIRECTIONS for making yarncraft flowers which follow are given below in lieu of repeating them in each specific set of directions.

Attaching Yarn Strands to Plastic Ring: Fold strand or strands in half. Using a crochet hook, pull folded end through ring to form a loop, then pull cut ends of the strand through this loop, pulling to tighten.

Combing Flowers to Fluff: Use a large plastic comb with both fine- and coarse-tooth sections. Using coarse-tooth section first, comb strands gently, beginning at the cut ends, then combing toward ring base until the plies of yarn are fused into a soft fluff. Run fine-tooth section of comb through fluff 2 or 3 times to smooth and finish, then proceed according to specific directions.

DAISY CARD AND FLOWER STRAND CARDS: See Chapter 10.

YARN BUTTON CENTERS FOR FLOWERS

Using worsted-weight yarn, double strand, a steel crochet hook #00, and a ½" plastic ring, work 12 single crochet sts through center and around ring. Fasten with a slip st to first single crochet made. Cut yarn and draw through loop. Pull cut end strands through sts on reverse side with crochet hook and trim close to sts.

YARNCRAFT FLOWERS

CHIFFON DAISY

See illustration on page 90.

Size: 3½" diameter.

Yarn: Medium-weight; knitting worsted or similar; 4 yards per daisy.

Flower Card: #2 (see Chapter 10).

Crochet Hook: Steel #00.

Additional Supplies: Plastic comb; plastic rings ¾" diameter; hair spray (super-hold or hard-to-hold type).

Cut 28 strands, each measuring 4". Attach 2 strands at a time to plastic ring. Comb lightly with coarse-tooth section of comb just enough to separate plies (do not comb to fluff). Trim excess fluff from around edge, if necessary. Spray lightly two or three times, allowing to dry each time. Fasten to fabric with button centers or as desired.

TWO-COLOR FLOWER

Size: 3¼" diameter.

Yarn: Knitting worsted or any similar yarn; about 3 yards each of 2 colors will make 1 flower.

Flower Card: #1 (see Chapter 10).

Crochet Hook: Steel #00.

Plastic Rings: ¾" outside diameter.

NOTE: All directions not specifically detailed below can be found in General Directions at the beginning of this chapter.

Cut 18 strands of Color A and 18 strands of Color B, each 3½" long. Attach 2 strands at a time of one color to one side of plastic ring, then attach 2 strands of the other color to opposite side of ring, as pictured on blouse with two-color flower trim (see page 92).

STRIPED FLOWER

See illustration on page 94.

Size: 3" diameter.

Yarn: Knitting worsted or any similar yarn; about 3 yards each of 2 colors.

Flower Card: #1 (see Chapter 10).

Crochet Hook: Steel #00.

Additional Supplies: Plastic rings, ½" outside diameter; hair spray of the super-hold or hard-to-hold type.

NOTE: All directions not specifically detailed below can be found in General Directions at beginning of this chapter.

Cut 16 strands each of 2 colors, each measuring 3½". Attach 2 strands at a time of one color to plastic ring, alternating colors, as shown in illustration of cardigan blouse with striped flower trim. Comb all strands to fluff. Trim excess fluff from around edge. Spray lightly two or three times, allowing to dry thoroughly each time.

LOOP DAISY

The loop daisy is most attractive when made with gift-tying yarn or super-bulky wool yarn; 6 yards of either of these yarns will make five 8-petal, four 10-petal, or three

12-petal loop daisies. When the extra-thick, gift-tying yarn is used, it is advisable to make 8-petal daisies; the super-bulky wool is more attractive made into 10- or 12-petal daisies. Cotton string and white fabric glue in an applicator-top container are needed to make these flowers.

Place an 8″ strand of cotton yarn or string in slot of daisy card (see Chapter 10). Wind cut end of yarn through slot, over and under one side of card, through slot, over and under other side of card, until there are 4 loops (petals) on each side of slot. This will make an 8-petal daisy. For a 10-petal daisy, wind 5 loops on each side of slot; for a 12-petal daisy, wind 6 loops on each side of slot. Cut yarn 1½″ from card and tuck cut ends into upper and lower loops to hold. Apply a small amount of glue along the vertical portion of yarn that has been passed in and out of slot. Tie cotton string in a single knot over glued portion. With thumbs, push loops (petals) on both sides carefully off card. Pull string tight and hold in this position a few seconds until glue has begun to set, then tie a second tight knot in string. Holding the 2 ends of string and the 2 cut ends of yarn all together, gently flatten petals in a circle (as shown in illustration of tote bag with loop daisy bouquet on page 95. Place on flat surface with cut ends up, allowing to dry 10 or 15 minutes before using. Trim cut ends of yarn and string to ½″. These loop daisies may be sewn to fabric with small pearls, flat buttons, or contrasting color yarn cross-stitch at centers.

KNITTED FLOWERS

BROWN-EYED SUSAN

See illustration on page 97.

Size: 5″ diameter.

Yarn: Knitting worsted; yellow, about 10 yards; cocoa or light brown, about 4 yards.

Crochet Hook: Aluminum size G.

Additional Material: Plastic rings 1⅛″ outside diameter.

NOTE: All directions not specifically detailed below can be found in General Directions at the beginning of this chapter.

Cut 60 strands of yellow, each 5½″ long. Attach 3 strands at a time to plastic ring. Cut 40 strands of brown, each 3½″ long. Tie these tightly tog in the middle with matching yarn. Pull tie ends through center of yellow daisy base, until tied middle of brown strands protrudes slightly from ring on reverse side. Using this as a shank, sew flower to fabric over knitted leaves, or as desired. For Knitted Leaves see pages 88–89.

FLORAL MOTIF

See also illustration on page 98.

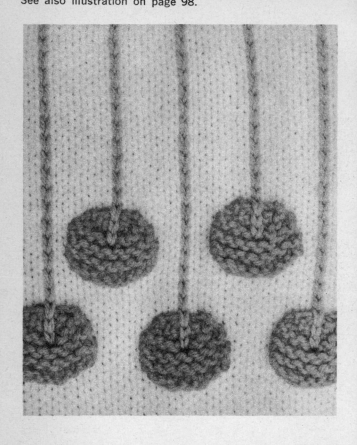

ALTERNATE FLORAL MOTIF

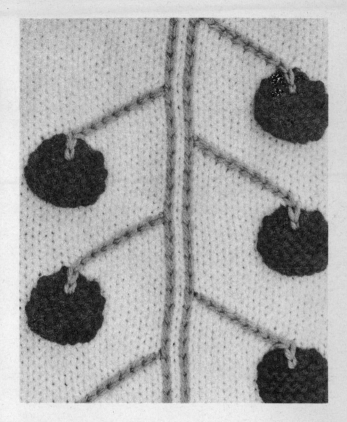

Motifs: Using #8 knitting needles and yarn of desired color, cast on 8 sts and knit across 8 rows. Slip the handle end of a steel crochet hook #00 through these 8 sts, then with hook end draw working yarn through all sts, pulling tightly. Cut yarn about 1" from loop, pull this end strand through loop on hook and pull tightly to fasten. With crochet hook, pull cut ends through purl sts on reverse side.

Stems: Pin each floral motif in position as shown or as desired, then work stem, using a yarn needle and the embroidery chain st (illustrated below), fastening top of floral motif to fabric with first 3 chain sts. Fasten end strands of chain st at each end by pulling through sts on reverse side. When it is necessary to thread a new strand of yarn through yarn needle while working chain st, complete a chain and insert needle through loop of chain to reverse side. Cut strand about 1½" from fabric and tie new strand with a firm knot close to fabric, taking care not to disturb the unanchored chain on right side.

EMBROIDERED CHAIN STITCH

Working from starting point toward you, as shown, insert yarn needle up through fabric; insert needle again at same place to back of fabric, then bring point of needle up again through next knit stitch, pulling working yarn upward so that loop (chain) just made will lie flat and snug against the fabric.

KNITTED LEAVES

See illustration on page 97.

Size: Each leaf, 5" long.

Yarn: Knitting worsted; about 1½ oz makes 4 leaves.

Knitting Needles: 1 pair #9 (or any size required to obtain the stitch gauge given on page 89).

Stitch Gauge: 8½ sts equal 2″ in Garter Stitch.

Make 4: Cast on 24 sts and knit across 1 row, then shape leaf as follows:

Row 1: K 1, sl 1, k 1, psso, knit across row to last 3 sts, k 2 tog, k 1 (how to slip a st and psso can be found in Chapter 8).
Rows 2, 3, and **4;** Knit.

Repeat these 4 rows until 6 sts remain on needles, completing through Row 4. On next row, k 1, sl 1, psso, k 2 tog, k 1. Last row: K 2 tog, k 2 tog. Knit the last 2 remaining sts tog. Cut yarn and draw through remaining st.

Using a yarn needle and strand of matching yarn, draw strand through cast-on sts at bases of all 4 leaves, pull into a tight circle and tie ends of strands securely. Block and allow to dry thoroughly.

QUICK AND EASY THINGS TO MAKE AND DECORATE

ELBOW-SLEEVE SHIFT WITH CHIFFON DAISY TRIM

Material Required: One shift made from directions in Chapter 2; 6 chiffon daisies on page 82; 6 buttons, $\frac{3}{8}''$ to $\frac{3}{4}''$ diameter; about 6 yards of green knitting worsted for stem; crochet hook, aluminum size G.

Using green yarn, double strand, crochet a chain about 45" long. Tack this chain in zigzag position down front of shift and attach a daisy at upper and lower ends of chain, and in each angle of chain, as shown, by sewing a button in each daisy center.

BLOUSE WITH TWO-COLOR FLOWER TRIM

Size: Directions are given first for 30"–32" bust measurement. Changes for larger sizes (34"–36", 38"–40") follow in parentheses. Proper size should be circled lightly in pencil throughout directions before beginning.

Yarn: Knitting worsted; 8 oz dark color, 4 oz light color.

Knitting Needles: 1 pair #8 (or any size required to obtain the stitch gauge given below).

Stitch Gauge: 9 sts equal 2".

Additional Materials: Two-color yarncraft flowers, 5 in matching yarn; 5 buttons for flower centers. (In the illustration, light-green yarn button centers were used. Directions for these can be found on pages 82–83).

BACK: Using dark color, cast on 73 (79, 85) sts and knit across 4 rows, then (beginning with a knit row) work in Stockinette Stitch until piece measures 14" from start. Shape sleeves: At beginning of next 2 rows (once each side) cast on 10 sts. When sleeves measure 6" (6½", 7"), and beginning on next reverse-side row, knit across 4 rows and bind off all sts (knitwise) on reverse side loosely.

LEFT FRONT: Using light color, cast on 33 (36, 39) sts and knit across 4 rows, then (beginning with a knit row) work in Stockinette Stitch until piece measures 14" from start. Shape left sleeve: At beginning of next right-side row, cast on 10 sts. When sleeve measures 6" (6½", 7"), and beginning on next reverse-side row, knit across 4 rows and bind off all sts (knitwise) on reverse side loosely.

RIGHT FRONT: Using dark color, cast on 41 (44, 47) sts and work as for left front until work measures 14″ from start. Shape right sleeve: At beginning of next reverse-side row, cast on 10 sts. Finish as for left front.

Use a half strand of yarn for all sewing.

Assembling and Finishing: Sew left and right front pieces tog on reverse side, using light color and running backstitch. Pick up 22 (25, 28) sts along each sleeve piece, using matching yarn, before assembling. Work in Garter Stitch until there are 2 purl ridges on right side of fabric, then bind off all sts (knitwise) on reverse side loosely. Sew upper sleeve and shoulder seams on reverse side, using overcast st and leaving a 9½" (10", 10") opening for neckline. Sew lower sleeve and side seams. Pin flowers down front seam at even intervals, as shown, and sew buttons to fabric through centers of flowers.

See pages 82–83 for Two-Color Flower trim directions.

CARDIGAN BLOUSE WITH STRIPED FLOWER TRIM

Materials Required: One cardigan blouse made from directions in Chapter 5; 3 striped flowers of desired contrasting colors; 3 strands bulky or super-bulky green yarn for stems, each about 12" long.

Placing the green yarn strands tog, tie a single knot close to one end, as shown. Clip the other ends to various lengths and pin on blouse as shown or as desired, tacking lightly on reverse side of fabric at knot and two or three places along yarn, using cotton sewing thread. Sew flowers to ends of strands, as shown.

See page 83 for Striped Flower trim directions.

TOTE BAG WITH LOOP DAISY BOUQUET

Materials Required: Tote bag made from directions in Chapter 1, unlined; loop daisies, 12-petal, 6 in contrasting color; 2 yards additional yarn, from which daisies have been made, for stems and bow; white fabric glue, with applicator top; glitter with shaker-top container (optional).

Place a sheet of foil inside tote bag to prevent glue from penetrating to back of bag. Cut 6 strands, each 10" long, for stems and bow. Place 4 strands tog and tie bow with remaining 2 strands, as shown. Glue bow, stems, and daisies in place, as shown. When thoroughly dry, remove foil and tack daisies and bow to inside of bag with cotton sewing thread. Decorate centers of daisies as desired or with glitter, as follows: Spread a drop of glue about ½" diameter in center of daisy, then carefully sprinkle a generous amount of glitter over the glue. Allow glue to dry thoroughly before moving tote bag. Sew in lining, if desired.

See pages 83–84 for Loop Daisy directions.

DECORATOR PILLOW WITH BROWN-EYED SUSAN MOTIF

Materials Required: One pillow in Stockinette Stitch, made from directions in Chapter 2; one Brown-Eyed Susan; one 4-leaf spray.

NOTE: Decorate pillow cover before inserting pillow form.

Place 4-leaf spray on pillow cover, as shown. Tack at center and at tip of each leaf with matching yarn. Sew Brown-Eyed Susan over center of leaf spray. Insert pillow form and finish according to directions.

See pages 84—85 for Brown-Eyed Susan directions.
See pages 88—89 for Knitted Leaves directions.

CAP-SLEEVE BLOUSE WITH FLORAL MOTIF

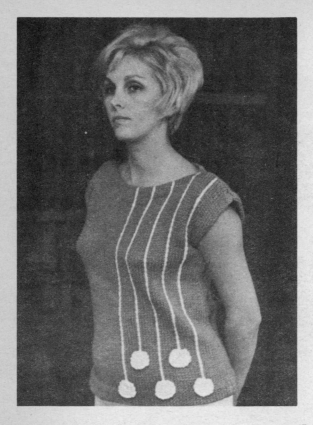

The cap-sleeve blouse in Stockinette Stitch, directions for which are given in Chaper 2, may be decorated as shown above or with the alternate arrangement of knitted floral motifs. A few yards of one or more colors of knitting worsted or similar yarn are sufficient for either of these motifs.

See pages 86–88 for Floral Motif.

Chapter 7

SURFACE WEAVING

Surface weaving is an easy and attractive way to decorate plain knitted items with small amounts of leftover yarns. As an applied decoration on a knitted fabric, it is so simple to do that only a close-up photograph of the pattern is necessary.

HOW TO START A SURFACE-WEAVE PATTERN

Determine the exact middle of the knitted fabric to be decorated, then weave the first row of pattern from the middle to the left edge, leaving enough yarn at the right to

99

weave back to the right-hand edge. When this is completed, as shown above, thread the strand of yarn remaining at the starting point in middle and weave in the opposite direction, back to the right edge. The right- and left-hand edges of pattern will now be exactly the same, and using this and close-up photo of pattern as a guide, the pattern can be worked from the right edge to the left edge on each pattern row. Always leave a 2″ strand of yarn at the right edge when beginning a surface-weave pattern, and clip working strand to 2″ length at left edge after each row is completed. These edge strands may be finished in one of two ways, depending upon the nature of the item being made. When no backing is needed for the item, these strands can be tied, two by two, in a firm double knot, then clipped to about ¾″ length. If a backing is to be used, steam press the end strands toward the middle of the fabric on the reverse side, clip to ¾″, and press iron-on fabric or fabric tape over these end strands. Apply the iron-on fabric or tape according to directions on the packet or instruction leaflet of manufacturer.

VARIOUS PATTERNS AND EASY ITEMS TO MAKE

WEAVER'S PATTERN

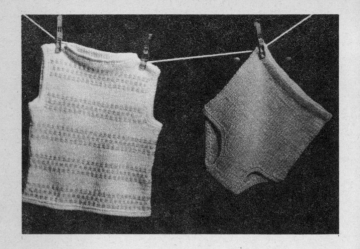

Size: Directions are given first for 1–2-year size (19" chest and hip measurements); changes for larger size (3–4 years; 20½" chest and hip measurements) follow in parentheses.

Yarn: Knitting worsted; 4 oz white and 4 oz contrasting color.

Knitting Needles: Size 1–2 years, use 1 pair #7 (or any size required to obtain the stitch gauge given below); size 3–4 years, use 1 pair #8 (or any size required to obtain the stitch gauge given below).

Stitch Gauge: #7 needles, 9½ sts equal 2".
#8 needles, 9 sts equal 2".

Crochet Hook: Steel #00.

Elastic: ½" wide, sufficient length for shorts waistline.

TOP: Back and Front are identical. **Make 2 of the following:** Using white, cast on 55 sts and work in Stockinette Stitch

until piece measures 7½" (8"). Shape arm openings: At beginning of next 2 rows (once each side), bind off 5 sts, then continue in Stockinette Stitch until arm openings measure 5" (5½") straight up from underarm. Bind off all sts loosely.

Assembling and Finishing: Steam press pieces lightly on reverse side and work surface-weave pattern, using contrasting color and following the close-up photo of Weaver's pattern as a guide. Sewing all seams with a half strand of yarn, sew shoulder seams on reverse side, using running backstitch and leaving a 6" opening for neckline. Turn neckline down into a crescent shape at front, with widest part measuring ¾", and sew. Sew side seams on right side, using flat stitch. Using white, work 2 rows single crochet around entire neckline, beginning and ending at center back; work 2 rows single crochet around arm openings and lower edge. Block to desired measurements. Tie end strands of surface-weave pattern on reverse side, as directed at beginning of this chapter.

SHORTS: Using contrasting color, cast on 48 sts and work in Stockinette Stitch for 7½" (8"), then bind off 2 sts at beginning of every row until 12 sts remain. Work until this 12-st section measures 1" (1½"), then increase 1 st at beginning and end of each right-side row until there are 24 sts on needles. At beginning of next 2 rows (once each side), cast on 12 sts and work over these 48 sts until piece measures 7½" (8") from the 12 sts cast on, on each side. Bind off all sts loosely.

Assembling and Finishing: Using a half strand of yarn, sew side seams in shorts. Sew a ½" hem at waistline, using overcast st and leaving a ¾" opening for insertion of elastic. Run proper length of elastic through this opening, fasten securely, and sew the ¾" opening closed. Work 2 rows of single crochet around leg openings. Block to desired measurements.

CHECKER PATTERN

Materials Required: Tote bag in Stockinette Stitch, unassembled, the directions for which can be found in Chapter 2; 2 oz super-bulky yarn in contrasting color for surface weaving; large plastic yarn needle.

Steam press bag lightly on reverse side. Using contrasting color, work surface weave in Checker pattern, following the close-up photo as a guide. Complete tote bag as directed.

DIAMOND-WEAVE PATTERN

Size: 14″ square.

Yarn: Super-bulky; 10 oz main color, 4 oz contrasting color.

Knitting Needles: 1 pair #10½ (or any size required to obtain the stitch gauge given below).

Stitch Gauge: 7 sts equal 2″.

Crochet Hook: Aluminum size G.

Additional Materials: One 14″ square pillow form (available at needlework shops and department store yarn sections); 1 large-eye plastic yarn needle for surface weaving.

Make 2 of the following: Using main color, cast on 40 sts and work in Stockinette Stitch for 14″. Bind off all sts loosely.

Assembling and Finishing: Steam press each piece lightly on reverse side and work Diamond-Weave pattern, following close-up photo, beginning first row as directed at beginning of this chapter. Block each piece separately. Steam press end strands of surface weave toward middle of fabric. Using contrasting color, work 1 row single crochet around all sides of each piece, working 3 single crochet sts in each corner. Holding reverse sides tog and using a half strand of yarn, sew these 2 edges tog around 3 sides, using overcast st through inside strands of single crochet sts. Insert pillow form and sew remaining edge of each piece tog.

NAVAJO PATTERN

SCATTER RUG IN NAVAJO PATTERN

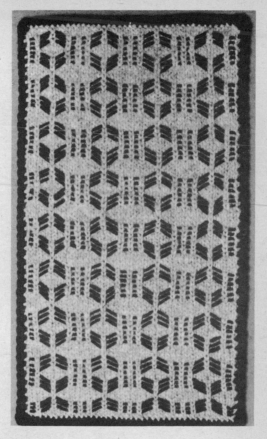

Size: Approximately 18″×28″.

Yarn: Super-bulky wool; 10 oz main color, 4 oz contrasting color.

Knitting Needles: 1 pair #11 (or any size required to obtain the stitch gauge given on page 110).

Stitch Gauge: 5 sts equal 2".

Crochet Hook: Aluminum size G.

Additional Material: Iron-on tape, 1½" width, or iron-on cloth for backing.

Using main color, cast on 42 sts and work in Stockinette Stitch until piece measures 28". Bind off all sts loosely. Work surface-weave pattern from close-up photo, beginning first row as directed at beginning of this chapter. Clip end strands to ¾" and steam press toward middle of fabric on reverse side. Work 2 rows single crochet around edges, using contrasting color and working 3 single crochet sts in each corner on each row. Press iron-on tape to edges on reverse side to hold strands, or back entire rug with iron-on cloth, following manufacturer's directions.

Size: Approximately 20"×30", exclusive of fringe.

Yarn: Super-bulky wool; 14 oz main color, 2 oz each of 3 contrasting colors for surface-weave pattern.

Knitting Needles: 1 pair #11 (or any size required to obtain the stitch gauge given below).

Stitch Gauge: 5 sts equal 2".

Crochet Hook: Aluminum size F or G for attaching fringe.

Additional Material: Iron-on tape, 1½" width, or iron-on cloth for backing.

Using main color, cast on 51 sts and work in Stockinette Stitch until rug measures 30". Bind off all sts loosely. Work surface-weave pattern from close-up photo, beginning first row as directed at beginning of this chapter. Use color 1 on the 3 straight-weave rows, color 2 next weave row, color 3 on next 2 rows, and color 2 on last row. Clip end strands to ¾" and steam press toward middle of fabric on reverse side. Press iron-on tape to edges of reverse side to hold strands, or back entire rug with iron-on cloth, following manufacturer's directions.

CHEROKEE DIAMOND PATTERN

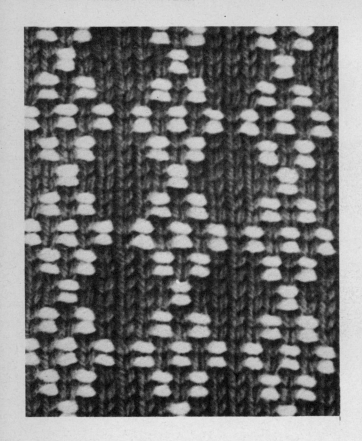

Size: Tote bag is given first in medium size (11"×12½"). Changes for larger size (13"×14½") follow in parentheses. Hat fits all women's head sizes.

Yarn: Super-bulky-type wool. Main color, 12 oz, contrasting color, 4 oz.

Knitting Needles: 1 pair #10½ (or any size required to obtain the stitch gauge given below) and 1 pair #11.

Stitch Gauge: Stockinette Stitch on #10½ needles, 7 sts equal 2".

Additional Material: ½ yard iron-on fabric for backing.

TOTE BAG: Using #10½ needles and main color, cast on 31 (37) sts and work in Stockinette Stitch for 1". Knit across next purl-side row for upper-edge hemline turn. Continue in Stockinette Stitch until piece measures 25" (29") above hemline-turn row. Knit across next purl-side row for corresponding upper-edge hemline turn. Continue in Stockinette Stitch for 1" and bind off all sts very loosely. Steam press lightly on reverse side and work surface-weave pattern, using contrasting color yarn and beginning first row as directed in the beginning of this chapter.

BRAIDED HANDLE: Using main color cut 15 strands, each approximately 60" long. Holding strands tog, tie a loose single knot in one end. Anchor this end firmly, divide into 3 groups of 5 strands each, and braid snugly to within 4" of end. Wrap a strand of yarn 3 times around end of braid and tie tightly. Untie knot at other end and tie the same. Wet braid thoroughly in lukewarm water, squeeze excess moisture out, and stretch flat on hard surface to about 53" length, exclusive of tassel ends. Allow to dry in this position. Trim tassels to 3".

Assembling and Finishing: Fold upper and lower edges down at hemline turn, then cut iron-on fabric backing to this exact size. Cut edge strands of surface weave to 1" and steam press away from edges and toward middle of bag on reverse side. Unfold hemline portion of bag on upper and lower edges; do not apply iron-on fabric to these edges. Pin bond side of iron-on fabric to reverse side of bag below hemline-turn rows, and bond to bag according to manufacturer's directions, making sure that all the surface-weave

116

end strands are underneath the iron-on fabric. Fold bag with hemline portions tog, and sew each side. Turn hem at upper edge and sew to iron-on fabric, using cotton sewing thread. Sew braid to side seams, as shown, using a half strand of yarn and sewing from outer edge of braid to middle, following the contours of the braided strands of yarn.

Hat: Using #11 needles and main color, cast on 61 sts and work in Stockinette Stitch for 2½″. Knit across next purl-side row for hemline turn. Continue in Stockinette Stitch for 2½″ above hemline-turn row, then change to #10½ needles and continue until piece measures 8″ above hemline-turn row. On next right-side row, *k 7, sl 2 (tog) knit-wise, k 1, pass these 2 sl sts (tog) over k st*. Repeat between *'s across row and end: K 1. Purl across next row. Work in Stockinette Stitch for 4 rows, then decrease again on right side as follows: K 1, *k 5, sl 2 (tog) knitwise, k 1, pass these 2 sl sts (tog) over k st*. Repeat between *'s across row. Purl across next row. Work in Stockinette Stitch for 2 more rows, then cut working yarn about 25″ from fabric, thread through a yarn needle and slip the stitches from knitting needle onto this strand. Work surface-weave design, beginning 2 rows below first decrease row made, working downward until 2 complete pattern units have been made. Pull strand of yarn holding upper edge sts into a closed circle and fasten securely on reverse side. Using a half strand of yarn, sew side edges tog. Tie surface-weave edge strands tog with a firm double knot and clip to ¾″ length. Turn brim at lower edge along hemline-turn row and sew to reverse side with a loose overcast st.

Blocking: Wet hat thoroughly in lukewarm water, squeeze out gently, and roll in terry-coth towel to take up excess moisture. Use a standard 2-lb coffee can as a block. Place 2 thicknesses of terry-cloth towel over can, and place hat over this block. Flatten crown against top of can. Flatten brim into a flange around edge of can and allow to dry thoroughly in this position before moving.

MORE SURFACE WEAVE PATTERNS

BALLOON PATTERN

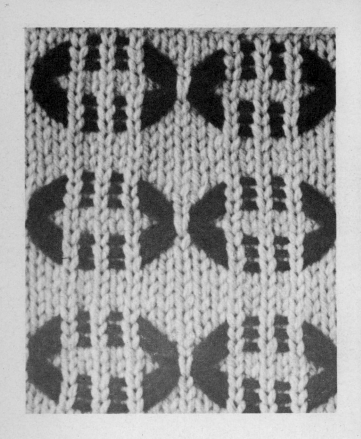

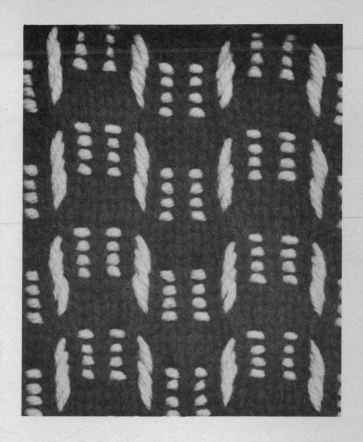

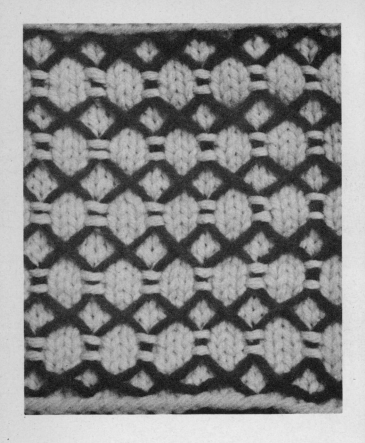

Knitted ground stitch: Cast on a multiple of 6 stitches plus 5.

Row 1: Knit.
Row 2: Purl.
Row 3: K 2, *p 1, k 2*. Repeat between *'s across row.
Row 4: Purl.
Row 5: Same as Row 3.
Row 6: Purl.

Surface-weave pattern: Using contrasting color yarn, weave pattern from upper to lower edge.

Part Three

LACY AND ELEGANT PATTERNS

Chapter 8

A COLLECTION OF BRIGHT NEW PATTERNS AND CREATIVE DESIGNS

NOTE: Instructions for special techniques and stitches precede the directions for each.

DOUBLE DECREASE

A simple double decrease is done by knitting or purling 3 stitches together as if they were one. This eliminates 2 stitches at one time from the row being worked, leaving one stitch on the needle where there were 3 on the previous row. For this double decrease, directions always state: Knit 3 together (k 3 tog) or purl 3 together (p 3 tog).

127

POMPEIAN LACE PATTERN

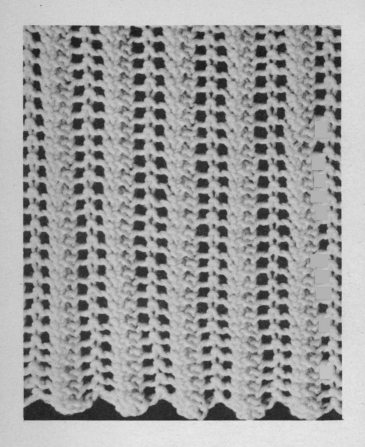

Cast on a multiple of 6 stitches plus 1.

Row 1: K 1, *o, k 1, k 3 tog, k 1, o, k 1*. Repeat between
*'s across row.
Row 2 (reverse side): Knit.

Size: Directions are given first for 34"–36" bust measurement. Changes for larger sizes (38"–40", 42"–44") follow in parentheses.

Yarn: Knitting worsted; blouse, 12 oz; shift, 20 oz.

Knitting Needles: Size 34–36, use 1 pair #8 (or any size required to obtain stitch gauge given below).

Size 38–40, use 1 pair #9 (or any size required to obtain stitch gauge given below).

Size 42–44, use 1 pair #10 (or any size required to obtain stitch gauge given below).

Stitch Gauge: Pattern Stitch on #8 needles, 8½ sts equal 2".

Pattern Stitch on #9 needles, 8 sts equal 2".

Pattern Stitch on #10 needles, 7½ sts equal 2".

Crochet Hook: Steel #00.

Front and Back are identical. **Make 2 of the following:** Cast on 79 sts and knit across 2 rows, then work in Pompeian Lace pattern until piece measures 13" (14", 14") for blouse or desired length from lower edge to underarm for shift.

SHAPE SLEEVES: Cast on 12 sts at beginning of next 6 rows (counting both front and reverse sides as rows), taking care to follow pattern. Continue over these 151 sts until sleeve measures 7½" (8", 8½") when measured straight up from underarm to upper edge. Complete pattern through Row 1 and bind off all sts (knitwise) on reverse side very loosely.

Assembling and Finishing: Sew upper-sleeve and shoulder seams on reverse side, using a half strand of yarn and overcast st, leaving a 9½" (10", 10") opening for neckline. Sew underarm and side seams. Work 3 rows single crochet around neckline, beginning and ending with a shoulder seam, and around lower edge of sleeves. Block to desired measurements.

HOW TO SLIP A STITCH

Insert right needle into stitch to be slipped, but instead of knitting or purling this stitch, slide it onto right needle without further action, then continue according to specific directions. Stitches are slipped knitwise throughout directions in this book unless purlwise is specifically stated. Generally, a stitch is slipped knitwise when it is to be passed over the next knit stitch, and slipped purlwise when it is to remain in sequence between other stitches across a row. The position of the working yarn is not changed when slipping a stitch unless specifically stated in directions.

HOW TO PASS SLIP STITCH OVER KNIT STITCH (psso)

With point of left needle, lift slipped stitch over knitted stitch and off the point of right needle. When directions state: k 2 tog, psso, the slipped stitch is lifted over the stitch remaining in exactly the same way. This is another type of double decrease which leaves one stitch on the needle where there were 3 on the previous row.

CAPRICE PATTERN

Cast on a multiple of 12 stitches plus 1.

Rows 1 and **2:** Knit.
Row 3: K 5, *o, sl 1, k 2 tog, psso, o, k 9*. Repeat between *'s across row, ending last repeat: k 5 (instead of k 9).
Row 4: Purl.
Row 5: P 3, *k 2, o, k 3, o, k 2, p 5*. Repeat between *'s across row, ending last repeat: p 3 (instead of p 5).

Row 6: K 2 tog, *p 11, k 3 tog*. Repeat between *'s across row, ending last repeat: k 2 tog (instead of k 3 tog).
Row 7: Same as Row 3.
Row 8: Knit.

DOUBLE THROW

Insert needle into stitch as if to knit, wrap yarn around needle 2 times and complete as for a knit stitch.

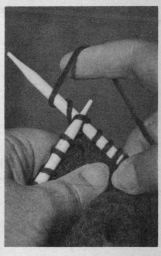

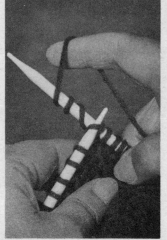

TRIPLE THROW

Work as for a double throw, wrapping yarn around needle 3 times.

133

QUADRUPLE THROW

Work as for a double throw, wrapping yarn around needle 4 times.

NOTE: A double, triple, or quadruple throw is always knitted into a stitch, differing from a 3-throw or a 4-throw, which is always worked between stitches.

TRIPLE-PURL PATTERN

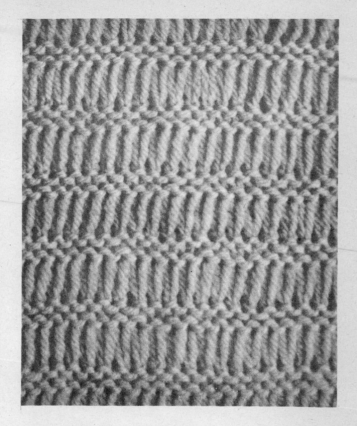

Cast on any number of stitches.

Rows 1 and **2:** Knit.
Row 3: K 1, knit a triple throw into each st across row.
Row 4: Knit, knitting first strand in each triple throw and dropping second and third strands from left needle without working.

LACY SEASHELL PATTERN

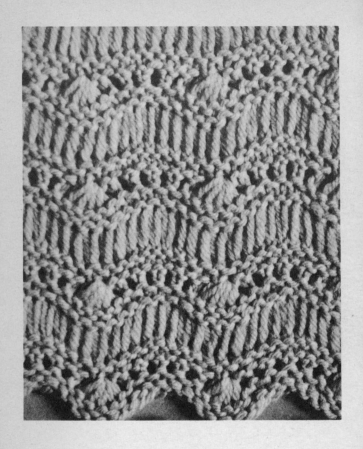

Cast on a multiple of 10 stitches plus 1.

Row 1 and **2:** Knit.
Row 3: *K 1, o, k 1, o, k 1, knit a double throw into each of the next 5 sts, k 1, o, k 1, o*. Repeat between *'s and end: k 1.
Row 4: K 5, *sl 5 purlwise (slip first strand, drop second strand from left needle without working), return to left needle and purl these 5 long sts tog, k 9*. Repeat between *'s across row, ending k 5 (instead of k 9).
Rows 5 and **6:** Knit.
Row 7: K 1, knit a triple throw into each st across row.
Row 8: Knit across row, knitting first strand of each triple throw and dropping second and third strands from left needle without working.

DOUBLE KNOT

Bring end of right strand or loop over and under left strand or loop, pull firmly in opposite directions, then repeat a second time, pulling ends firmly in opposite directions until a snug knot is formed between strands or loops.

TWO-COLOR BOWS PATTERN

It is suggested that knitting worsted and #9 needles be used for this pattern.

RIGHT-HAND SIDE (facing in photo): Using color A, cast on any desired number of stitches. Row 1 is front of fabric; Row 2 is reverse side.

Row 1: Knit across row to last 2 sts, knit a quadruple throw into next st, k 1.
Row 2: K 1, knit a st into st directly below quadruple throw, slip quadruple throw from left needle without working, and to front of fabric. Knit to end of row. Repeat above 2 rows for desired length.

LEFT-HAND SIDE (facing in photo): Using color B, cast on any desired number of stitches. Row 1 is front of fabric; Row 2 is reverse side.

Row 1: K 1, knit a quadruple throw into next st, knit to end of row.
Row 2: Knit across row to last 2 sts, knit a st into st directly below quadruple throw, slip quadruple throw from left needle without working, k 1. Repeat above 2 rows for the same length as right-hand side.

TIE BOWS: Place loop edges of fabric tog. Insert knitting needle into first loop of each color and pull up sharply. Tie these 2 loops into a firm double knot, pulling each color loop on second tie toward contrasting color fabric, as shown. Repeat this procedure at each pair of loops until entire length of each piece of fabric has been joined.

SQUARE KNOT

Bring end of right strand or loop over and under left strand or loop, pulling ends firmly in opposite directions, then bring end of left strand or loop over and under right strand or loop, pulling the ends firmly in opposite directions until a snug knot is formed between strands or loops.

3-THROW

Bring working yarn between points of needles from knit position at back, around right needle and again to the back, 3 times. Each time yarn passes between points of needles is counted as one throw. A 3-throw is always done between stitches.

4-THROW

Bring working yarn between points of needles from knit position at back, around right needle and again to the back, 4 times. Each time yarn passes between points of needles is counted as one throw. A 4-throw is always done between stitches.

LACY BOWS PATTERN

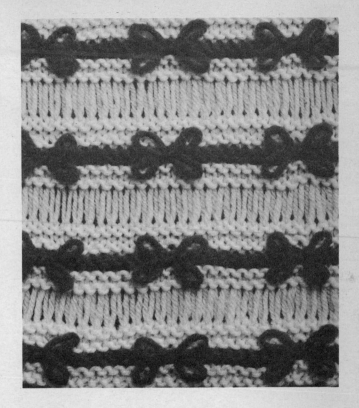

Cast on a multiple of 11 stitches, using main color. It is suggested that knitting worsted and #9 or #10 needles be used for this pattern.

Row 1: (Main color) Knit.
Row 2: (Main color) Knit.
Row 3: (Drop main color, attach contrasting color, double strand) Knit.

Row 4: (Contrasting color, double strand) K 5, *3-throw, k 1, 3-throw, k 10*. Repeat between *'s across row, ending last repeat: k 5 (instead of k 10).

Row 5: (Cut contrasting color; pick up main color) Knit across row, slipping all 3-throws from left needle and to front of work.

TIE BOWS: Insert free needle through a pair of loops and pull up sharply; repeat with each pair across row. Tie each pair of loops tog in a firm square knot, as shown.

Rows 6, 7, and **8:** (Main color) Knit.

Row 9: (Main color) K 1, k a triple throw into each st across row.

Row 10: (Main color) Knit, knitting first strand of each triple throw and dropping second and third strands from needle without working.

FLORET BORDER

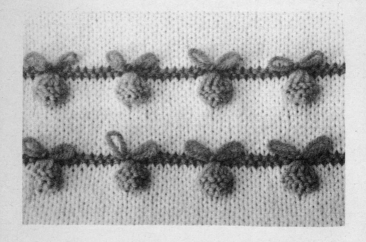

Cast on a multiple of 10 stitches plus 1, and knit in Stockinette Stitch, using main color, for desired length before beginning pattern.

Row 1: K 5, *break main color and attach a pastel color, tying with a firm double knot which rests snug against back of needle, and work a floret, as follows: (k 1, p 1, k 1, p 1, k 1) in next st before slipping it from left needle; turn work to reverse side and k 5; turn work to right side and k 5; turn work to reverse side and k 5; turn work to right side and knit a double throw into each of these 5 sts; break pastel color, attach main color, k 9*. Repeat between *'s across row, alternating each of 2 pastel colors, and ending last repeat: k 5 (instead of k 9).
Row 2: P 5, *sl 5 purlwise (slip first strand, drop second strand), p 9*. Repeat between *'s across row, ending last repeat: p 5 (instead of p 9).
Row 3: Drop main color, attach green, k 5, *k 5 tog, k 9* Repeat between *'s across row, ending last repeat: k 5 (instead of k 9).
Row 4: K 5, *4-throw, k 1, 4-throw, k 9*. Repeat between *'s across row, ending last repeat: k 5 (instead of k 9).
Row 5: Cut green, pick up main color, k 5, *drop 4-throw from left needle and to front of work, k 1, drop 4-throw from left needle and to front of work, k 9*. Repeat between *'s across row, ending last repeat: k 5 (instead of k 9).

TIE BOWS: Insert free needle through a pair of loops and pull up sharply; repeat with each pair across row. Tie each pair of loops tog in a firm square knot, as shown.

Row 6: Purl across row, using main color, then continue Stockinette Stitch to desired length.

Size: Directions are given first for size 30″–32″ bust measurement. Changes for larger sizes (34″–36″, 38″–40″, 42″–44″) follow in parentheses. It is suggested that the proper size be circled lightly in pencil throughout directions before beginning.

Yarn: Knitting worsted; white, 12 oz; light green, 1 oz; light rose, 1 oz; light blue, 1 oz.

Knitting Needles: 1 pair #8 (or any size required to obtain the stitch gauge given on page 145).

Stitch Gauge: 9 sts equal 2".

NOTE: Directions are given for Floret Border on both front and back of blouse; however, border may be omitted on back, if desired.

Front and Back are identical. **Make 2 of the following:** Using white, cast on 71 (81, 91, 101) sts and knit across 4 rows, then (beginning with a knit row) work in Stockinette Stitch for 1½". Work Floret Border pattern, Rows 1 through 6. Work in white for 1½", then work Floret Border once more. Continue in white until work measures 14" (14", 15", 15") from start. Shape sleeves: At beginning of next 2 rows, cast on 10 sts (once each side). When work measures 2" above sleeves, work Floret Border, Rows 1 through 6. Work in white for 1½" and work Floret Border once more. Continue in white until sleeves measure 6" (6½", 7", 7½"), and beginning on next reverse-side row, knit across 4 rows and bind off all sts (knitwise) on reverse side loosely.

Sleeve Edging: Sew shoulder seams, using a half strand of yarn and leaving a 9½" opening for neckline. With reverse side facing, pick up 47 (50, 53, 56) sts along sleeve edge. Knit across 5 rows and bind off all sts (knitwise) on reverse side loosely.

Assembling and Finishing: Sew underarm and side seams. Block to desired measurements.

SLIP-CLUSTER

This interesting stitch is more formidable to read than to do, and when done one step at a time is surprisingly easy. When one or two slip-clusters have been worked, the rest can be done without further reference to directions for working them. They are made from triple-throw stitches made on the previous row with a regular knit stitch between, which serves as an anchor. To work a slip-cluster, *bring yarn forward (toward you, between points of needles), insert right needle purlwise into the first strand (of triple throw) without working, and slip it from left needle onto right needle (creating a long stitch that has been slipped). Repeat this until 5 long stitches have been slipped onto right needle, then take yarn (between points of needles) to back of work (away from you), slip all the long stitches back onto left needle, yarn to front (between points of needles), slip long stitches to right needle, yarn to back (between points of needles), slip long stitches to left needle, yarn to front of work (between points of needles), slip long stitches to right needle, yarn to back (between points of needles)* and a slip-cluster has been made. Be sure that yarn has been pulled rather snugly around long stitches each time it passes between points of needles. Repeat between *'s each time a slip-cluster is called for in specific directions.

TWO-COLOR DAISY CHAIN PATTERN

Cast on a multiple of 6 stitches plus 1, using the colored yarn.

Row 1: (Color) K 1, *knit a triple throw into next 5 sts, k 1*. Repeat between *'s across row.
Row 2: (Color) K 1, *slip-cluster next 5 sts, k 1*. Repeat between *'s across row.
Row 3: (Color) Knit, taking care to knit each st in each slip-cluster.
Row 4: (Color) Knit.
Row 5: (White) Knit.
Row 6: (White) Purl.
Row 7: (White) Knit.
Row 8: (White) Purl.
Rows 9 and 10: (Color) Knit.
Row 11: (Color) K 4, *knit a triple throw into next 5 sts, k 1*. Repeat between *'s across row and end: k 3.
Row 12: (Color) K 4, *slip-cluster 5, k 1*. Repeat between *'s across row and end: k 3.
Rows 13 and 14: (Color) Knit.
Row 15: (White) Knit.

Row 16: (White) Purl.
Row 17: (White) Knit.
Row 18: (White) Purl.
Rows 19 and 20: (Color) Knit.

CARDIGAN IN TWO-COLOR DAISY CHAIN PATTERN

Size: Directions are given first for 32"–34" bust measurement. Changes for larger sizes (36"–38", 40"–42") follow in parentheses.

Yarn: Knitting worsted; 12 oz white, 8 oz contrasting color.

Knitting Needles: 1 pair #6 for ribbed collar and cuffs and 1 pair #10 (or any size required to obtain the stitch gauge given below).

Stitch Gauge: Pattern stitch on #10 needles, 19 sts equal 4".

Crochet Hook: Steel #00.

Additional Materials: 4 small pearl buttons.

BACK: Using contrasting color and #10 needles, cast on 85 (91, 97) sts and work in Two-Color Daisy Chain pattern, changing from color to white, as indicated, for 14" (15", 15"). On next 2 white rows, bind off 12 sts (once each side for sleeve insets). When sleeve insets measure 7" (7½", 8"), bind off all sts loosely on a white row.

LEFT FRONT: Using contrasting color and #10 needles, cast on 43 (43, 49) sts and work in pattern, beginning with Row 11 through last row of pattern stitch, then repeating from Row 1 thereafter for 14" (15", 15"). At beginning of next white knit row, bind off 12 sts for sleeve inset. When sleeve inset measures 5½" (6", 6½"), bind off 9 sts at beginning of next purl row for neckline, then decrease 1 st at neck edge 3 times, taking care to keep continuity of pattern. When sleeve inset measures 7" (7½", 8"), bind off all sts loosely on a white row.

RIGHT FRONT: Work as for left front, placing sleeve inset and neckline on opposite sides, to correspond with left front.

SLEEVES: Sew shoulder seams, using a half strand of yarn. Using #10 needles, and with right side facing, pick up 61 (67, 67) sts along vertical shoulder edge. (Do not pick up sts over the 12 horizontal bound-off sts of front and back.) Knit across 1 row, using color (reverse side), then work in pattern for approximately 12", ending with a completed motif row in color. Change to #6 needles and white, and work in k 1, p 1 ribbing for 4" (or desired length). Bind off all sts loosely, knitting the knit sts and purling the purl sts.

COLLAR: Using white and #6 needles, cast on 92 (96, 96) sts and work in k 1, p 1 ribbing for 4". Bind off all sts loosely.

Assembling and Finishing: Using half strand of yarn, sew side seams; sew upper portion of each edge of sleeve to vertical bound-off sts, then sew sleeve seams tog to lower edge. Using white, work 1 (2, 2) row(s) single crochet along right-center front edge, then work 2 buttonhole rows, spacing the 4 buttonholes evenly from upper edge, as shown, and as directed in Chapter 5. Work 1 (2, 2) more row(s) of single crochet on this edge to complete. Work 4 (5, 5) rows of single crochet along left-center front edge. Sew 4 buttons along this edge to correspond to buttonholes. Pin bound-off sts of collar evenly around neckline and sew, as shown. Block to desired measurements.

Chapter 9

MORE PRETTY PATTERNS AND THINGS TO MAKE

EYELET LACE PATTERN

Cast on an odd number of stitches.

Rows 1 and **2:** Knit.
Row 3: K 1, *o, k 2 tog*. Repeat between *'s across row.
Rows 4, 5, and **6:** Knit.
Row 7: K 1, knit a triple throw into each stitch across row.
Row 8: Knit, knitting first strand of each triple throw and dropping second and third strands from left needle without working.

TOGA TOP OR SHIFT IN EYELET LACE PATTERN

Size: Directions are given first for 32"–34" bust measurement. Changes for larger sizes (36"–38", 40"–42") follow in parentheses.

Yarn: Lightweight wool sports yarn or any similar wool yarn yielding the proper stitch gauge; toga top, 10 oz; shift, 18 oz.

Knitting Needles: 1 pair #6 (or any size required to obtain the stitch gauge given below).

Stitch Gauge: 21 sts equal 4" of pattern.

NOTE: This item may also be done in Triple Purl or Thalia patterns provided the proper size knitting needle is used to obtain stitch gauge given above.

Back and Front are identical. **Make 2 of the following,** making sure that both back and front contain the same number of pattern units: Cast on 89 (99, 109) sts and work in Eyelet Lace until piece measures 20" (21", 22") for toga top or desired length from shoulder seam to lower edge for shift; complete pattern through Row 1 and bind off all sts (knitwise) on reverse side loosely.

Assembling and Finishing: Sew shoulder seams, leaving a 9½" (10", 10") opening for neckline. Sew side seams, leaving a 6½" mandarin slit at lower edges, as shown, and 6¾" (7", 7½") arm openings. Block to desired measurements.

152

153

THALIA PATTERN

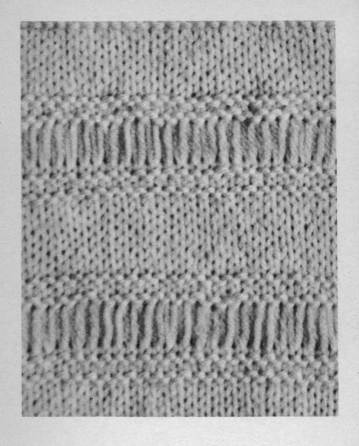

Cast on any number of stitches.

Rows 1 and **2:** Knit.
Rows 3, 4, 5, 6, 7, 8, and **9:** Work in Stockinette Stitch (knit right side, purl reverse side), beginning and ending with a knit row.
Rows 10, 11, and **12:** Knit.
Row 13: K 1, knit a triple throw into each st across row.
Row 14: Knit, knitting first strand of each triple throw and dropping second and third strand from left needle without working.

Repeat Rows 1 through 14 for pattern, and end upper edge: work Rows 1 through 11, then bind off all sts (knit-wise) on reverse side.

CORINTHIAN LACE PATTERN

Cast on a multiple of 4 stitches plus 1.

Row 1 (reverse side): K 1, *o, k 3, o, k 1*. Repeat between
*'s across row.
Row 2: P 2, *p 3 tog, p 3*. Repeat between *'s across row
and end last repeat: p 2 (instead of p 3).
Row 3: Purl.
Row 4: Knit.

PLACE SETTING MAT IN CORINTHIAN LACE PATTERN

Size: Approximately 12½"×18".

Yarn: Hand-knitting cotton, quick-knit/crochet cotton, or any similar yarn yielding the proper gauge; 4 oz.

Knitting Needles: 1 pair #7 (or any size required to obtain the stitch gauge given below).

Stitch Gauge: 11 sts equal 2" of pattern.

Crochet Hook: Steel #1.

Cast on 85 sts and work in Corinthian Lace until mat measures about 12" from start. Complete pattern st through Row 3 and bind off all sts. Work 3 rows single crochet around all sides, working 3 single crochet sts in each corner on each row. Launder and allow to dry, then steam press lightly on reverse side. Spray starch may be used, if desired, following manufacturer's directions on container.

ZIGZAG LACE PATTERN

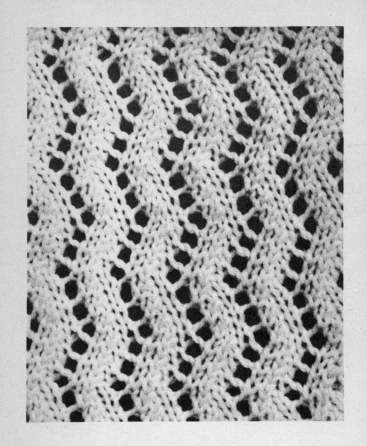

Cast on a multiple of 4 stitches plus 1

Row 1: K 2, *o, k 1, k 2 tog, k 1*. Repeat between *'s across row, ending last repeat: k 2 tog.
Row 2 (and all even-numbered rows): Purl.
Rows 3 and **5:** Same as Row 1.

Row 7: *K 2 tog, k 1, o, k 1*. Repeat between *'s across row, ending last st: k 1.

Rows 9 and **11:** Same as Row 7.

Row 12: Purl.

CARRIAGE COVER IN ZIGZAG LACE PATTERN

Size: Approximately 22"×34", exclusive of fringe.

Yarn: Lightweight; baby yarn or any similar yarn yielding the proper stitch gauge; 7 oz.

Knitting Needles: 1 pair #8 (or any size required to obtain the stitch gauge given on page 160).

Stitch Gauge: 14 sts equal 3″ in pattern.

Crochet Hook: Steel #1.

NOTE: This item may also be made in Triple Purl, Thalia, Corinthian Lace, Eyelet Lace, Caprice, Alpine Stripe, or Popcorn Lace patterns.

Cast on 97 sts and work in Zigzag Lace pattern for 32″. Complete pattern to last-numbered row and bind off all sts loosely.

Finishing: Steam press edges lightly on reverse side. Work 1 row single crochet around all sides, working 3 single crochet sts in each corner.

Fringe: Cut strands of matching yarn each 3½″ long. Fold 2 strands tog and pull folded end through single crochet st with crochet hook to form a small loop. Pull cut ends through loop end and pull to tighten. Repeat in each single crochet st around all sides, as shown.

Blocking: Zigzag Lace pattern has a tendency to slant slightly on the bias before blocking. Block to size, pinning at 2″ intervals, making sure that carriage cover is pinned to exact rectangular shape. Allow to dry throughly before removing pins.

POPCORN LACE PATTERN

Cast on a multiple of 4 stitches plus 1.

Row 1 (right side): P 1, *o, p 3, o, p 1*. Repeat between *'s across row.

Row 2: K 2, *p 3 tog, k 3*. Repeat between *'s across row, ending last repeat: k 2 (instead of k 3).

Row 3: P 2, *o, p 1, o, p 3*. Repeat between *'s across row, ending last repeat: p 2 (instead of p 3).

Row 4: P 2 tog, *k 3, p 3 tog*. Repeat between *'s across row, ending last repeat: p 2 tog (instead of p 3 tog).

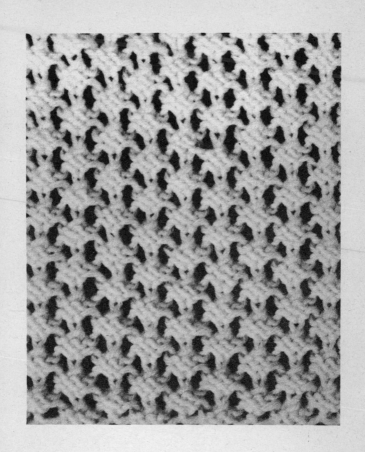

ALPINE STRIPE PATTERN

Cast on a multiple of 8 stitches plus 1.

Rows 1 and **2:** Knit.
Row 3: K 3, *k 2 tog, o, k 6*. Repeat between *'s across row, ending last repeat: k 4 (instead of k 6).
Row 4: Purl.
Row 5: K 2, *k 2 tog, o, k 1, o, sl 1, k 1, psso, k 3*. Repeat between *'s across row, ending last repeat: k 2 (instead of k 3).
Row 6: Purl.
Row 7: K 1, *k 2 tog, o, k 3, o, sl 1, k 1, psso, k 1*. Repeat between *'s across row.
Row 8: Purl.
Row 9: K 2 tog, *o, k 1, o, sl 1, k 2 tog, psso*. Repeat between *'s across row, ending last repeat: sl 1, k 1, psso.
Rows 10, 11, and **12:** Knit.
Rows 13, 14, 15, 16, and **17:** Work in Stockinette Stitch (knit right side, purl reverse side), beginning and ending with a knit row.
Row 18: Knit.

SHELL BORDER PATTERN

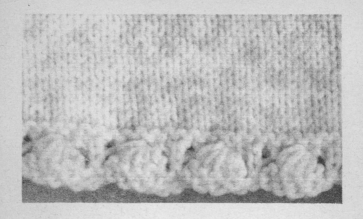

Cast on a multiple of 6 stitches plus 1.

Row 1: K 1, *o, k 5, turn work to reverse side and k 5, turn work to right side and knit a double throw into these 5 sts, o, k 1*. Repeat between *'s across row.
Row 2: K 1, *o, k 1, sl 5 purlwise (slip first strand, drop second strand), return to left needle and purl these 5 sts tog, k 1, o, k 1*. Repeat between *'s across row.
Row 3: Knit.
Row 4: Knit.

End of Shell Border; continue in Stockinette Stitch or desired pattern.

GIRL'S BLOUSE WITH SHELL BORDER PATTERN

Size: Ages 4 and 5

Yarn: Knitting worsted or any similar yarn yielding the proper stitch gauge.

Knitting Needles: For 4-year size, use 1 pair #8 (or any size required to obtain the stitch gauge below). For 5-year size, use 1 pair #9 (or any size required to obtain the stitch gauge given below).

Stitch Gauge: Stockinette Stitch on #8 needles, 9 sts equal 2".
Stockinette Stitch on #9 needles, 8½ sts equal 2".

BACK: Cast on 55 sts loosely and work Shell Border, Rows 1 through 4, then work in Stockinette Stitch until work measures 8". Sleeves: At beginning of next 6 rows cast on 3 sts. Work over these 73 sts until sleeve measures 5" straight up from underarm. Bind off all sts loosely.

FRONT: Work as for back until sleeve measures 3½". Shape neckline: on next right-side row, k 25, bind off next 23 sts, knit to end of row. Working each shoulder separately, k 2 tog at neck edge only on every right-side row 3 times. When sleeve measures 5", bind off remaining 22 sts loosely.

NECKLINE TRIM: Cast on 85 sts loosely and work Shell Border, Rows 1 through 3, then bind off all sts knitwise on reverse side.

SLEEVE TRIM: Make 2. Cast on 43 sts and work as for neckline trim.

Assembling and Finishing: Using a half strand of yarn, sew shoulder, sleeve, and side seams; sew Shell Border trim to neckline and lower edges of sleeves. Block to desired measurements.

CHANFRON PATTERN

Cast on a multiple of 5 stitches plus 1.

Rows 1 and **2:** Knit.
Row 3: K 1, knit a triple throw into each st across row.
Row 4: *K 1 (knit first strand, drop second and third strands from needle); leaving yarn at back (away from you), sl 4 purlwise (slip first strand, drop second and third strands from left needle), return these 4 long sts to left needle, insert point of right needle in space directly under left needle to the left of 4th long st, wrap yarn once around right needle and complete as for a knit st, leaving long sts on left needle. Bring yarn forward between points of needles, slip all 4 long sts onto right needle purlwise without working, yarn to back*. Repeat between *'s across row, ending last st: k 1.
Row 5: *K 4, k 2 tog*. Repeat between *'s across row and end: k 1.
Rows 6, 7, and **8:** Knit.

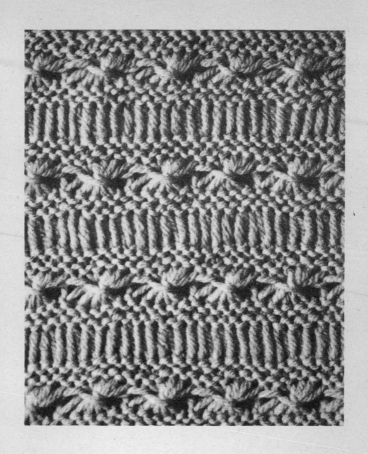

Row 9: Same as Row 3.
Row 10: Knit across row, knitting first strand of each triple throw and dropping second and third strands from left needle.

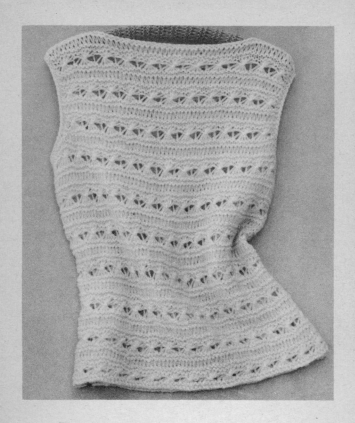

Size: Directions are given first for 32"–34" bust measurement. Changes for larger sizes (36"–38", 40–42") follow in parentheses.

Yarn: Knitting worsted; 12 oz.

Knitting Needles: 1 pair #9 (or any size required to obtain the stitch gauge given below).

Stitch Gauge: Pattern stitch, 8 sts equal 2".

Crochet Hook: Steel #00.

NOTE: This item can also be made in Triple Purl or Thalia patterns, provided the proper size needles are used to obtain the stitch gauge given above.

Back and Front are identical **Make 2 of the following:** Cast on 71 (76, 81) sts and work in Chanfron pattern for 14" (15", 15"). Shape arm openings: At beginning of next 2 knit rows, bind off 10 sts (once each side). Continue in pattern until arm openings measure 6½" (7", 7½"). Complete pattern through Row 1, and bind off all sts (knitwise) on reverse side loosely.

Assembling and Finishing: Using a half strand of yarn, sew shoulder seams on reverse side, using overcast st and leaving a 9½" (10", 10") opening for neckline, as shown; sew side seams on right side, using flat stitch and taking care to match pattern rows. Work 1 row of single crochet around arm openings. Block to desired measurements.

Cast on a multiple of 13 stitches plus 2.

Rows 1 and 2: Knit.
Row 3: K 1, knit a triple throw into each st across row to last st and end: k 1.
Row 4: K 1, *sl 3 sts purlwise (slip first strand, drop second and third from needle), return to left needle, bring yarn forward, and insert right needle purlwise through back strands of all 3 loops and (p 1, k 1, p 1, k 1, p 1, k 1) into these 3 loops before slipping them from left needle; sl 7 sts, return to left needle and purl them all tog; yarn to back, sl 3, return to left needle and insert needle knitwise into front of strands of all 3 loops and (k 1, p 1, k 1, p 1, k 1, p 1) into these 3 loops*. Repeat between *'s across row and end: k 1.
Rows 5, 6, 7, and 8: Knit.
Row 9: K 1, knit a triple throw into each st across row.
Row 10: Knit, knitting first strand and dropping second and third strands from needle.

Cast on a multiple of 12 stitches plus 1.

Row 1: K 2, *o, sl 1, k 1, psso, p 2, k 1, p 2, k 2 tog, o, k 3*. Repeat between *'s across row, ending last repeat: k 2 (instead of k 3).
Row 2: Purl.
Row 3: K 2 tog, *o, k 2, p 2, (k l, p 1, k 1, p 1) into next st before slipping from left needle, turn work to reverse side and k 4, turn work to right side and k 4, turn work to reverse side and k 4, turn work to right side and k 4, p 2, k 2, o, sl 1, k 2 tog, psso*. Repeat between *'s, ending last repeat: sl 1, k 1, psso.
Row 4: P 6, *p 4 tog, p 11*. Repeat between *'s across row, ending last repeat: p 6 (instead of p 11).
Row 5: Same as Row 1.
Row 6: Purl.
Row 7: K 2 tog, *o, k 2, p 2, k 1, p 2, k 2, o, sl 1, k 2 tog, psso*. Repeat between *'s across row, ending last repeat: sl 1, k 1, psso.
Row 8: Purl.

COUNTERPOINT PATTERN

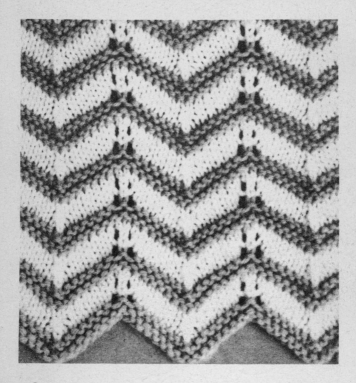

Cast on a multiple of 16 stitches plus 1, using Color A.

Rows 1 and **2:** (Color A) Knit.
Row 3: (Color B) K 1, *o, k 6, sl 2 knitwise (tog), k 1, psso (tog), k 6, o, k 1*. Repeat between *'s across row.
Row 4: (Color B) Purl.
Row 5: (Color B) Same as Row 3.
Row 6: (Color B) Purl.
Rows 7 and **8:** (Color A) Knit.

All knitters are extremely fond of making stoles in lacy or unusual pattern stitches, and following are two sets of general directions by which stoles can be knitted in any one of a number of selected patterns, instructions for which are in this and the preceding chapter.

Size: Approximately 19½" wide (after blocking); 63" long, exclusive of fringe.

Yarn: Knitting worsted; 16 oz.

Knitting Needles: 1 pair #10 (or any size required to obtain the stitch gauge given below).

Stitch Gauge: 15 sts equal 4" in pattern.

Crochet Hook: Steel #00.

Patterns with no definite upside-down direction can be used for straight one-piece stoles. Patterns with a definite upside-down direction should be made in two pieces and seamed down the center back.

The number of stitches to be cast on varies according to pattern stitch used. A group of patterns suitable for stoles is listed below; following each pattern is the chapter in which it appears, whether one or two pieces, and the number of stitches to be cast on.

Pompeian Lace, Chapter 8, two pieces, 67 sts
Caprice, Chapter 8, one piece, 61 sts
Triple-Purl, Chapter 8, one piece, 61 sts
Lacy Seashell, Chapter 8, two pieces, 61 sts
Lacy Bows, Chapter 8, one piece, 66 sts
Eyelet Lace, Chapter 9, one piece, 61 sts
Thalia, Chapter 9, one piece, 66 sts
Corinthian Lace, Chapter 9, two pieces, 65 sts
Zigzag Lace, Chapter 9, one piece, 65 sts
Popcorn Lace, Chapter 9, one piece, 65 sts
Alpine Stripe, Chapter 9, two pieces, 65 sts
Chanfron, Chapter 9, two pieces, 61 sts
Belamine Lace, Chapter 9, two pieces, 67 sts
Bavarian Lace, Chapter 9, two pieces, 61 sts
Counterpoint, Chapter 9, one piece, 65 sts

One-Piece Stole

Work in pattern until stole measures approximately 61½" long; complete pattern unit to last-numbered row or as necessary, and bind off all sts loosely.

Two-Piece Stole

Make 2: Work in pattern until piece measures approximately 31" long; complete pattern unit to last-numbered row or as necessary, and bind off all sts loosely. With right sides of fabric tog, sew stole pieces tog at bound-off edges.

Crocheted Edge (optional): Work 1 or 2 rows of single crochet along lengthwise edges or around entire edge area of stole, depending on the nature of the pattern selected. When working single crochet around all 4 sides, work 3 single crochet sts in each corner on each row.

Fringe (optional): For short (2") fringe, cut strands of yarn, each 4" long. For long (4") fringe, cut strands 8" long. Fold a strand in half and pull folded end through first st on width edge to form a small loop, using crochet hook. Pull cut ends through loop, then pull cut ends sharply to tighten. Repeat in each st across the 2 width edges of stole.

QUICK AND EASY CAP-SLEEVE SHIFTS

Easy and attractive cap-sleeve shifts can be made from the foregoing list of patterns, as well as the patterns on the following pages, in the same way that the two-piece stole is made. It is advisable, however, to buy 4 oz additional knitting worsted and use a size smaller needle. To determine the number of stitches to be cast on, make a stitch-gauge swatch (see Chapter 1), using the yarn and needles that will be used to make the garment. Using a metal tape measure or ruler, determine the exact number of stitches to 1" of fabric. Measure bust or hips (whichever measurement is larger), then divide the number of inches in this measurement in half. Now multiply this number (half of bust or hip measurement inches) times the number of stitches to 1″ of knitted fabric. The result will be the approximate number of stitches to be cast on. Adjust this number of stitches to the pattern multiple. For example: if the result of your figures shows that 68 stitches should be cast on, and the multiple of the desired pattern stitch is 10 plus 1, add 3 stitches. The total number of stitches to be cast onto 1 side of the shift will now be 71. Up to 4 or 5 stitches can be added in order to adjust to the number of stitches in pattern multiple. If a loose-fitting shift is desired, then another stitch multiple can be added. Work in pattern until piece measures desired dress length, measured from shoulder seam to lower edge, bearing in mind that lacy or triple-throw patterns often drop 2″ or 3″ after being blocked. When both pieces have been completed, place right sides together and sew shoulder seams, leaving a 9½″ opening in middle for neckline. Sew side seams, leaving a 7″, 7½″, or 8″ opening each side for arms. Work 2 rows single crochet around neckline and arm openings. Lower edge can be finished with 2 rows of single crochet or hemmed. Block to desired measurements.

LACY BOBBLE BORDER PATTERN

Cast on a multiple of 10 stitches plus 1.

Row 1: P 5, *(k 1, p 1, k 1, p 1) in next st before slipping from left needle, turn to reverse side and k 4, turn to right side and k 4, turn to reverse side and k 4, turn to right side and lift 2nd, 3rd, and 4th st, one at a time (in that order) over first st and off left needle, k 1 (this is the remaining st of the 4 just worked), p 9*. Repeat between *'s across row, ending last repeat: p 5.
Row 2 (and all even-numbered rows): Purl.
Row 3: P 1, *o, p 2, p 2 tog, k 1, p 2 tog, p 2, o, p 1*. Repeat between *'s across row.
Row 5: P 2, *o, p 1, p 2 tog, k 1, p 2 tog, p 1, o, p 3*. Repeat between *'s across row, ending last repeat: p 2.
Row 7: P 3, *o, p 2 tog, k 1, p 2 tog, o, p 5*. Repeat between *'s across row, ending last repeat: p 3.
Rows 8, 9, and **10:** Purl.

End of border. Continue in Stockinette Stitch for desired length.

COTILLION PATTERN

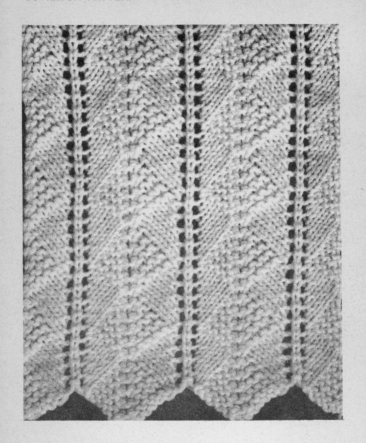

Cast on a multiple of 15 stitches.

Row 1: *P 2 tog, p 4, k 1, o, k 1, o, k 1, p 4, p 2 tog*. Repeat between *'s across row.
Row 2 (and all even-numbered rows): Purl.
Row 3: *P 2 tog, p 3, k 2, o, k 1, o, k 2, p 3, p 2 tog*. Repeat between *'s across row.
Row 5: *P 2 tog, p 2, k 3, o, k 1, o, k 3, p 2, p 2 tog*. Repeat between *'s across row.
Row 7: *P 2 tog, p 1, k 4, o, k 1, o, k 4, p 1, p 2 tog*. Repeat between *'s across row.
Row 9: *P 2 tog, k 5, o, k 1, o, k 5, p 2 tog*. Repeat between *'s across row.
Row 10: Purl.

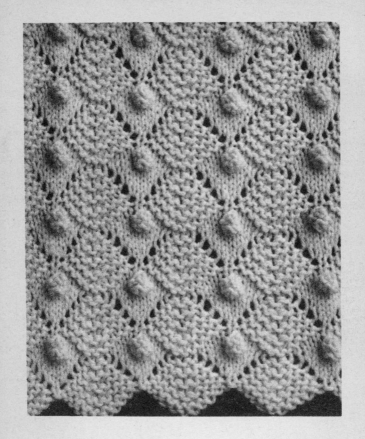

Cast on a multiple of 11 stitches.

Row 1: P 5, *k 1, p 10*. Repeat between *'s across row, ending last repeat: p 5.
Row 2 (and all even-numbered rows): Purl.
Row 3: *P 2 tog, p 3, lift increase knitwise, k 1, lift increase knitwise, p 3, p 2 tog*. Repeat between *'s across row.
Row 5: *P 2 tog, p 2, lift increase knitwise, k 3, lift increase knitwise, p 2, p 2 tog*. Repeat between *'s across row.
Row 7: *P 2 tog, p 1, lift increase knitwise, k 5, lift increase knitwise, p 1, p 2 tog*. Repeat between *'s across row.
Row 9: *P 2 tog, lift increase knitwise, k 3, (k 1, p 1, k 1, p 1) in next st before slipping from left needle, turn work to reverse side and k 4, turn work to right side and lift 2nd, 3rd, and 4th st, one at a time (in that order) over first st and off left needle, k 1 (this is the remaining st from the 4 just worked), k 3, lift increase knitwise, p 2 tog*. Repeat between *'s across row.
Row 10: Purl.

BAVARIAN DIAMOND PATTERN

Cast on a multiple of 15 stitches.

Row 1: P 3, *k 4, (k 1, p 1, k 1, p 1) in next st before slipping from left needle, turn to reverse side and k 4, turn to right side and k 4, turn to reverse side and k 4, turn to right side and lift 2nd, 3rd, and 4th st, one at a time (in that order), over first st and off left needle, k 1 (this is the st remaining from 4 just worked), and a bobble has been made; k 4, p 6*. Repeat between *'s across row, ending last repeat: p 3.
Row 2 (and all even-numbered rows): Purl.
Row 3: P 3, *k 2, k 2 tog, o, k 1, o, sl 1, k 1, psso, k 2, p 6*. Repeat between *'s across row, ending last repeat: p 3.
Row 5: P 3, *k 1, k 2 tog, o, k 3, o, sl 1, k 1, psso, k 1, p 6*. Repeat between *'s across row, ending last repeat: p 3.
Row 7: P 3, *k 2 tog, o, k 5, o, sl 1, k 1, psso, p 6*. Repeat between *'s across row, ending last repeat: p 3.
Row 9: P 3, *work a bobble in next st, k 7, work a bobble in next st, p 6*. Repeat between *'s across row, ending last repeat: p 3.
Row 11: P 3, *k 1, o, sl 1, k 1, psso, k 3, k 2 tog, o, k 1, p 6*. Repeat between *'s across row, ending last repeat: p. 3.
Row 13: P 3, *k 2, o, sl 1, k 1, psso, k 1, k 2 tog, o, k 2, p 6*. Repeat between *'s across row, ending last repeat: p 3.
Row 15: P 3, *k 3, o, sl 1, k 2 tog, psso, o, k 3, p 6*. Repeat between *'s across row, ending last repeat: p 3.
Row 16: Purl.

FLEURETTE PATTERN

Cast on a multiple of 17 stitches.

Row 1: P 4, *k 2 tog, k 2, o, k 1, o, k 2, sl 1, k 1, psso, p 8*. Repeat between *'s across row, ending last repeat: p 4.
Row 2 (and all even-numbered rows): Purl.
Row 3: Same as Row 1.
Row 5: P 4, *k 4, (k 1, p 1, k 1) into next st before slipping from left needle, turn to reverse side and k 3, turn to right side and k 3, turn to reverse side and k 3, turn to right side and lift 2nd and 3rd st, one at a time (in that order) over first st and off left needle, k 1 (this is the st remaining from the 3 just worked) and a bobble has been made; k 4, p 8*. Repeat between *'s across row, ending last repeat: p 4.
Row 7: Same as Row 1.
Row 9: P 4, *k 2, work a bobble in next st, k 3, work a bobble in next st, k 2, p 8*. Repeat between *'s across row, ending last repeat: p 4.
Row 10: Purl.

Part Four

FLOWER CARD DIAGRAMS

DAISY CARD DIAGRAM

Chapter 10

HOW TO MAKE DAISY AND FLOWER CARDS

Trace Daisy and Flower Card diagrams and transfer tracing to a piece of heavy cardboard. Cut out each card around diagram lines. These cards are then used according to specific directions for flowers in Chapter 6 and for fringe.

DAISY CARD DIAGRAM

Use for 8-, 10-, or 12-petal daisies. Directions for making loop daisies can be found in Chapter 6.

FLOWER CARD 1

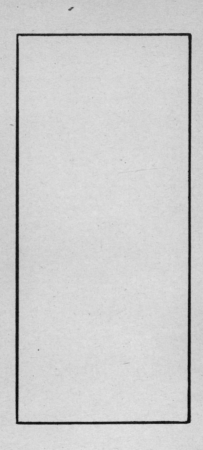

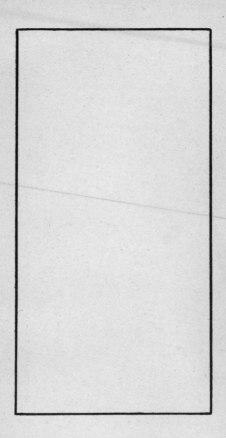

Flowers and fringe requiring strands of yarn to be cut 3½" or 4" long can be made without the aid of the flower cards; however, these cards are simple to make and speed up the process of flower or fringe making.

Flower Card 1 makes strands 3½" long. Flower Card 2 makes strands 4" long.

Wind yarn around width of card very loosely (to avoid stretching), beginning with cut end of yarn at lower edge. Wind yarn around card once for each strand of yarn required in any specific set of directions, and end with the second cut yarn end also at lower edge of card. Run scissors blade under all strands at lower edge of card, and cut through all of these strands.